Royal Horticultural Society

SMALL GARDEN
HANDBOOK

Royal Horticultural Society

SMALL GARDEN
HANDBOOK

Making the most of your outdoor space

Andrew Wilson

Special photography Steven Wooster

MITCHELL BEAZLEY

For Mum and Dad, who always said, 'Just do your best; we can't expect anything more.'

RHS Small Garden Handbook
Andrew Wilson

First published in Great Britain in 2013 by Mitchell Beazley,
an imprint of Octopus Publishing Group Ltd, Endeavour House, 189 Shaftesbury Avenue,
London WC2H 8JY
www.octopusbooks.co.uk

An Hachette UK Company
www.hachette.co.uk

Published in association with the Royal Horticultural Society, London

ISBN 978 1 84533 681 3

A CIP record of this book is available from the British Library.

Packaged by Griffin Books
Commissioning Editor Helen Griffin
Publishers Lorraine Dickey, Alison Starling
Art Director Jonathan Christie
Senior Art Editor Juliette Norsworthy
Designer Lizzie Ballantyne
Copy-editor Joanna Chisholm
Picture Research Manager Giulia Hetherington
Production Controller Peter Hunt
Proofreader Annelise Evans
Indexer Michele Clarke
RHS Publisher Rae Spencer-Jones
RHS Consultant Editor Simon Maughan

Set in DIN and Glypha

Printed and bound in China

The Royal Horticultural Society is the UK's leading gardening charity dedicated to advancing
horticulture and promoting good gardening. Its charitable work includes providing expert advice
and information, training the next generation of gardeners, creating hands-on opportunities for
children to grow plants, and conducting research into plants, pests and environmental issues
affecting gardeners. For more information, visit: www.rhs.org.uk or call 0845 130 4646.

Contents

Introduction

There is no definition of small that is – well – definitive, it would seem. The *Oxford English Dictionary* helpfully says 'not large', but perhaps it is this comparative quality that is important. Although the history of small gardens is also comparative in tone, what is certain is that the concept of smallness in respect of the garden is shrinking with each successive generation of gardeners.

This represents a challenge to our wellbeing. The need to wind down in the privacy of our gardens through productive and regular gardening, outdoor entertaining or simple relaxation will therefore require ever more inventive solutions.

RHS Small Garden Handbook addresses these issues of privacy and the productive use of a small space. It identifies your needs and offers realistic planting suggestions. This book aims to teach you how to look at your garden with a designer's eye and how to assess and quantify what you currently own. You can then combine this knowledge with your plans and inspirations to discover how best your small garden might be exploited.

Help is provided with careful planning guidance and forward thinking, enabling your ambition to be realistically and positively channelled. The book will help from the start of the project to the detailed choices for materials and appropriate species that will complete the garden. Guidance on maintenance and management is also included to enable the garden to evolve sustainably into the future.

This illustrated handbook with its easy visual references provides an indispensable support to the creation and development of your small garden projects. Practical and achievable case studies help to underpin each chapter, and design references point you towards other gardens that might support your thinking and crystallize decision-making about your own plot.

Enjoy the journey of discovery and the fulfilment that comes from the exploitation and development of even the smallest of spaces – gardens that reflect your personality and lifestyle.

◀ **Aim to be adventurous** by using bold foliage and lively colour, even in a small space. Containers of all kinds can be used to refresh the garden and introduce new ideas.

It is always worth allocating an area in which to relax. You can then sit there enjoying the surroundings and basking in its special atmosphere.

SMALL GARDEN

BASICS

When dreaming about your ideal garden you may well imagine the space to be much larger than it is in reality. Therefore when you actually come to design it, you should devote time to information gathering about the real situation and to organizing your thoughts if your garden is to be successful.

The intention is to identify and implement the most effective solutions, much in the way a professional designer would process information and possibilities. Fortunately there is also plenty of room for subjective and heart-based ideas and sentiment to surface during this planning process.

15 ways to... reveal your plot's potential

1. Measure your plot

Ensure that you have accurate dimensions for your garden. Use a retractable tape that is 5m (16ft) or longer and keep measurements as exact as possible. Record dimensions methodically.

2. Check the levels

Note any alterations in height within the garden. The level changes might be easy to measure if steps are already constructed, but in a sloping garden look at how the levels alter against garden boundaries or use a string line to assess the slopes.

3. Identify existing features

Record any major features such as storage areas, trees, beds and borders and the extent of any paving. The measurements and location of these elements will help you to decide what you want to keep or remove.

4. What soil do you have?

When assessing your garden's soil you need to establish its pH, which indicates its acidity or alkalinity. This measure tells you which plants are suitable for the soil. Inexpensive soil-testing kits are available from garden centres and online.

5. Is your soil healthy?

Gardens that are being converted from paved or neglected sites often have poor soil. Dig the soil thoroughly, incorporating nutrient-rich organic matter. In some cases new topsoil may be needed, but ensure first that drainage is good. Gardens that have

6. Pinpoint the character

Some gardens have an inherent sense of character. This may be related not only to how sunlight and shade work within the space but also to the age, surroundings and the hard and soft materials found within the plot. Take some time to decide on the elements that are important to the personality of your garden and how best you should exploit them.

been worked regularly and planted with care should have much better soil conditions.

7. Dig a little deeper

Although a new garden may appear troublefree it is a good idea to see what lies beneath the surface. Builders often leave their detritus on site covered by only a thin layer of soil. The original soil might also be compacted and need rotavation or aeration.

8. Tackle troublesome plants

Neglected, overmature or rampant plants and weeds should be pruned hard or removed altogether.

9. Note existing materials

Identify and assess the quality and character of the hard materials in your garden. Older properties often include brick or stone walls and concrete

13. Whose is the fence?

Check on the ownership of your boundaries. Some neighbours will not want you to attach anything, such as an awning, to the boundaries they own. Others may be keen to share the cost of renewal. More than two owners may be involved.

14. Planning a roof plot

Check on weight loadings for your roof before planning any form of planting, especially if you are considering the conversion of an old flat roof. In such areas, plants are grown in containers or raised planters, but soil can be very heavy so use soilless potting composts.

paving. Decide first what the material is and then on its condition and what you may need to do about it.

10. Can you borrow views?

Small areas can feel bigger if longer views or nearby vegetation can be successfully exploited, while less desirable views can be screened with carefully sited planting. Such considerations can have a significant impact on your design.

11. How private is your plot?

Small gardens are often overlooked by neighbouring properties. Although people have different tolerance thresholds for such exposure, it is useful to record those parts of your garden that are most open to public gaze and those where some degree of privacy can be found. Again this information may influence your eventual redesign of the garden.

12. Track the sun's arc

Identify how the sun moves across your garden both in a typical day and across the year. In winter when the sun is lower some small gardens will be in permanent shade. This affects what and where you plant.

15. Look before you lop

Check with your local authority before you do any major work. If your garden lies within a conservation area there may be limitations on what you can do. Trees over certain heights can only be removed after permission is granted.

Getting to know your plot

Before you start to do anything with your garden it is essential that you take time to find out what exactly you are responsible for. You need to take stock of its character and contents. Most designers divide this assessment into survey and analysis.

Survey information

Such an assessment is always factual and objective, but can include a wide range of information, from historical fact-finding to the size and type of brickwork used in the boundary walls.

Analysis information

This information is always subjective and based on your personal responses or feelings about the garden. It may include a perception of the garden's character or a sense of comfort or wellbeing when you are in the garden. Sometimes this feeling or response develops over time as you become familiar with the space and how it changes over the year.

The wait-and-watch approach

Some people advise that little is done to a garden for the first year so that you can watch and discover what treasures emerge, such as spring bulbs or autumn colours.

By using this approach to understanding your garden you will be in a better position to make informed and considered decisions.

How to log the results

When getting to know a garden it is invaluable to use a notebook or sketch pad in which to collect information and record your thoughts. Photographs of the garden at different times of the day or year can be helpful in reminding you of how things change during the seasons.

Alternatively, such a logging job can be done electronically. The advantage of this is that you can access digital imagery and do internet research. Simple software packages allow you to create and add measured plans, while metric graph paper has a grid on which you can draw out your measurements and start to redesign the garden layout.

▲ **The level of privacy** in a garden can affect how comfortable you feel using it. Careful choice of boundaries and screen planting will help conceal adjacent properties.

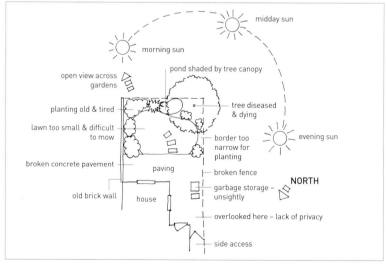

midday sun

morning sun

pond shaded by tree canopy

open view across gardens

tree diseased & dying

planting old & tired

lawn too small & difficult to mow

border too narrow for planting

evening sun

broken concrete pavement

paving

broken fence

NORTH

garbage storage – unsightly

old brick wall

house

overlooked here – lack of privacy

side access

▲ SIMPLE , HAND-DRAWN PLAN

Draw a layout plan of your garden including all the main features. Watch the way the sun affects the garden and analyse the extent of the shade. This will vary both daily and across the year. Explore the views out of the garden and the way in which neighbours might invade your privacy.

When you take over a well-established garden you are likely to assume responsibility for several plants that are new to you. By recognizing their key features you can more readily identify them and research how to care for them.

Measuring your plot

Before making more detailed measurements, always identify and measure your boundaries and the footprint of the property in which you live as it relates to the garden. Simple, hand-drawn layouts produced to scale will enable you to start assessing the space. Scales of 1:20 or 1:10 are best for small plots.

The house

The house walls are likely to be the most accurately built and provide the ideal baseline for measuring. Note the lengths of each wall, the location of windows, doorways, steps and finally drainpipes and vents. Look at how the walls meet and if there are angled or curved architectural features on the building itself.

The boundaries

Record how the boundaries relate to the building, their heights and arrangement. Few boundaries will be straight. Start measuring from the house with a central line. All measurements should be perpendicular to this line.

The changes in level

Once you have drawn out the boundaries and the basic layout of the garden you can add any level changes to the plan. Steps and walls are easily measured, but more organic slopes are harder to plot. By using a gardening line or string with a spirit level (and an assistant to help) you can measure the height differences at each corner of your plot and at significant locations.

If you wish to create a level surface, even seemingly insignificant level changes can add up to a great deal of earth movement in a small garden. The ideal is to balance any excavated soil with areas that need the levels to be raised or filled.

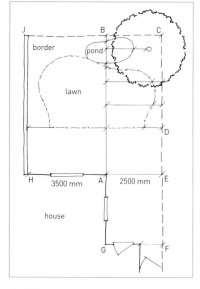

▲ SKETCH OF PLOTTING THE GARDEN

The garden is divided by straight, perpendicular lines, known as offsets. Careful measurement will identify inaccuracies and the exact geometry of your garden.

The planting

Measure the planting areas and significant trees and shrubs. Pinpoint their trunks on the plan as well as their canopy spread (and therefore the shade they cast). Finally measure the location and height of any buildings in your garden. This will also help in assessing the way shade is cast.

DIY DESIGN

Measuring made easy

Knowing the dimensions of your garden will help in quantifying its potential and scope, as the measurements are added to your plan. This is generally a job for two.

• Use a tape measure 25m (80ft) or 30m (100ft) in length, and a shorter rectractable one.
• Measure the façade of the house and its windows and doors as a basis, then do the boundaries.
• Take diagonal dimensions as check measurements. Boundaries are rarely straight.
• For odd-shaped plots, set up a straight line perpendicular to the house and take a series of 90° offset measurements at regular intervals to the boundaries.

Understanding your soil

In your garden, soil performs two main roles. The first is to support paving and any hard surface or structure that you introduce into the garden, while the second is to provide a fertile growing medium for your plants.

Soil has a fertile humus top layer (which can be 10–50cm/4–20in deep) and a subsoil one beneath. By digging a hole or trench you will be able to see the humus layer – generally dark and textured in quality. The subsoil is a mineral-rich, inorganic layer that can be very deep. It is often paler in colour than topsoil and contains stones, flints and coarser particles.

Most soils can be classified according to their clay, sand and silt content. Loam soil is a combination of all three in roughly equal measure.

Soil under hardscaping

Subsoil is a much better basis than topsoil for construction, although it may need to be compacted as part of the construction process to ensure that it provides a firm support. Therefore you should remove the fertile humus layer of soil in areas that are to be paved or have foundations for walls and fences. Store this topsoil for later use in any planting borders.

It is important when digging lower trenches for foundations that the subsoil and humus are not mixed because this will lower the overall fertility of the soil.

Clay soil

This soil often causes the most problems for gardeners. It bakes hard in summer and can shrink and crack as a result. In wetter periods clay soil retains moisture and becomes sticky and difficult to work. The increased water content makes it swell.

▲ **Soil often becomes compacted** and so will need to be prepared thoroughly before planting can start. This is especially important in new gardens.

Ironically many clay soils are also nutrient-rich but this is inaccessible to most plants until the physical structure of the soil is broken down. The addition of organic matter such as well-rotted manure, compost or leafmould can help to change the soil structure. Coarse grit or fine gravel has a similar effect. The hard work of opening the soil structure by digging is best done in winter, because frost can help to break down the structure too. Crops such as potatoes can also aid this breakdown process and provide food as a bonus.

Sometimes water puddles on the soil surface, and when wet the temperature of clay is significantly lower than other soil types. Alleviate this by installing a soakaway or perforated pipes below the surface. Backfill with free-draining soil or gravel.

Sandy soil

Sandy soil has an open, free-draining texture so there are few problems with drainage or standing water. It is well aerated but nutrient-poor, because the nutrients readily leach through its freely draining structure. The regular addition of well-rotted manure, compost or leafmould helps to improve soil structure as well as to retain nutrient levels and moisture content.

▲ **Clay soils swell when wet** and shrink or crack when dry. Such soils are difficult to work and poor drainage can be a major problem.

▲ **Sandy soils are free-draining** and leach nutrients so are easily exhausted. Often they are naturally acidic.

▲ **Silty soils are fertile** but suffer from poor drainage because their fine particles stick together and block water flow.

Silty soil

This is often very fertile but its fine structure often impairs drainage so it needs aeration and cultivation to break it up. As with other soils, organic matter and grit will help to improve silty soil structure.

Loamy soil

Loam soil, which is often considered the ideal, combines the main benefits of clay, sandy and silty soils. It has good fertility and an ability to retain some moisture as well as drain well.

◀ **Rhododendrons grow in acid soils** and go yellow and appear unhealthy in alkaline soils. Yew, box, lavender and thyme prefer alkaline soils. A local walk will show the species typical of your neighbourhood.

Loamy soil is easier to cultivate. The addition of organic matter maintains its fertility and open texture, for optimum root penetration.

Soil pH

The chemical character of the soil, which is measured by pH, depends on the original parent rock from which the soil is derived. Soils vary from acidic (below pH7) to alkaline (above pH7), with a balanced middle ground, which is termed neutral. The optimum range for good plant growth is pH 5.5–7.5.

Chemically neutral soils support the widest range of vegetation, with many plants that prefer slightly acid and slightly alkaline soil sharing the same conditions. Sandy soils tend to be acidic in nature, while soils in limestone areas are generally alkaline. Clay soils can be acid or alkaline.

The inherent quality of soil is virtually impossible to change and over the long term all soils will revert to type if left to themselves. It is therefore the best policy to accept the chemistry of your soil and choose plants that enjoy those conditions. To find out the pH level of the soil in your

garden, send a sample to a specialist laboratory or buy a soil-testing kit. Humus layers will vary in depth, but a sample taken 15–20cm (6–8in) below ground level will provide an accurate pH reading. Alternatively, there are soil maps that provide information on the soil type in your area.

Plants reveal pH

The plants that thrive naturally in your garden and neighbourhood are known as indicator species as they tell you the soil type, so what you can grow.

Access for materials

Many small urban gardens are inaccessible from the street either because they are part of a high-rise building or because the house or apartment has no additional external path or gate. Early in your planning it is worth remembering that soil excavations, clearance and demolition materials must go through the house or possibly in the lifts. Material will have to be bagged for easy movement and you will need to protect the furnishing and finishes in your home. This can add significant amounts of time to your plan.

Aspect & climate

Your garden's aspect is defined by its position relative to the sun, and in the northern hemisphere it is related to the position of due north. Its aspect is a vital indication of how it interacts with sunlight, wind and local climate.

Position of a garden wall

Walls, trees, garden buildings and the house all cast shade.

In the northern hemisphere, a garden wall facing north will be cold and shaded, while a south-facing one will be in full sun for most of the day and will not cast shadows.

East-facing walls catch the first sun of the morning, and in the summer this does not create problems. In the winter and spring however any early sun will raise temperatures quickly. If temperatures were at or below freezing during the night, then plants growing on or against the wall may be damaged, especially if this process is repeated over a number of days.

West-facing walls receive the last of the sun each day and are therefore the slowest to warm up, because the temperature will generally have risen gradually before the sun reaches this part of the garden.

Garden microclimates

The way in which sun and shade move across a garden, together with air movement in and around that space, create a garden's microclimate. In the northern hemisphere, gardens facing northwest, north and northeast will be significantly cooler during a typical year than those facing southwest, south and southeast.

Gardens surrounded by walls and fences are protected from wind, but those on high-level balconies or rooftops suffer more from wind exposure than almost any other except coastal plots. This is an invisible aspect of microclimate that can severely affect plant growth.

▲ **Clematis thrive in a sunny spot,** so check on the aspect and orientation of your garden before planting such sun-lovers in an appropriate part of the plot.

DIY DESIGN

Crown lifting

- You can carry out 'crown lifting' to reduce areas of heavy shade from trees and larger shrubs that have become overdense as they mature.
- Ideally crown lifting should be undertaken before a tree matures because the wounds will be smaller in size.
- Remove the lower branches so there is more space between the ground and the base of the canopy (as shown right). This allows greater accessibility beneath the branches, and the increased light improves planting conditions near the tree or shrub.
- When pruning a branch always make the cut just before the swollen base, where it joins the main stem. This will deter disease and rotting in the trunk.

Getting to know your plants

When you inherit a mature garden it is important to identify all the existing plants. The best way to do this is to compare key characteristics against plant photos in a good-quality, seasonally arranged encyclopedia.

Trees

These are identified most easily by their bark, leaf shape, flower or fruit. The bark is recognizable at any time of the year, but you will often have to wait until spring or summer to observe other obvious characteristics. However some trees such as ash or horse chestnut have specific winter bud formations that can be noted.

Shrubs

Shrubs are generally categorized by their foliage, flower and fruit, although some also bear decorative bark or branches. Some shrubs are invaluable because they flower in winter.

Perennials

Perennials are often much more difficult to identify as they die back in winter and some virtually disappear. It is therefore sensible to wait until summer before making decisions about many of these plants, as most species will have shown themselves by then.

TREES FOR SMALL GARDENS

These small and medium-sized trees may need pruning to keep them in shape.

1. Japanese maple (*Acer palmatum*) is compact, with good autumn colour and delicate leaves, in a range of cultivars.

2. Silver birch (*Betula pendula*) is elegant, with silver bark, small leaves casting light shade and high wildlife value.

3. Myrobalan plum (*Prunus cerasifera*) bears small flowers – it is often one of the first into flower; foliage matures to dark purple-red.

4. Cultivated crab apple (*Malus* 'John Downie') is a small tree offering spring blossom and long-lived, colourful, edible autumn fruit.

5. Fossil tree (*Ginkgo biloba*) often grows tall but with a narrow crown; this deciduous conifer casts light shade.

6. Sydney golden wattle (*Acacia longifolia*) is a winter-flowering tree with delicate foliage and a transparent crown casting light shade.

7. Cultivated pear (*Pyrus* 'Beurré Hardy') is typical of many fruit trees because it is now available on a variety of rootstocks and can be trained against a wall.

Evaluating your hardscaping

Within your garden you may find a mixture of hard materials and so need help in deciding which to keep and which to remove. As with your inherited plants you need to consider whether you like the hardscaping and whether each one fits your design criteria. Assess the character and the quality of the paving and also research how much you need for your new design. Be warned: it is difficult to match new with existing paving, which will have weathered.

Reusing materials

Natural paving such as sandstones and limestones are a pleasure to inherit, as are the more traditional sandstones. Small amounts of paving can be reused for seating bases or paved areas, but it is frequently better to start a new terrace with new material. Concrete may have been poured *in situ* (in which case it will form a large expanse with few joints) or have been precast into units to imitate natural stone.

Bricks, if they fit with your local vernacular, can work well when reused for paths and walls.

MATERIALS FOR SMALL SPACES

1. Natural stone comes in a mixture of slab sizes and stone types (here seen with slate, limestone and granite). Gravel can be matched to stone types and coloration.

2. Porphyry setts are available in many different colours; porphyry is an igneous rock that is often grainy and crystalline in character.

3. The contrasts in colour and dimensions between brick and stone form interesting patterns and break up the scale of the garden.

4. Handmade bricks and tiles can be combined for decorative effect for garden paving; check both materials for frost hardiness.

5. Limestone can be laid in large slabs as a formal edge to a lawn or as a path in heavily used areas of the garden. Limestone is available in a range of colours.

Imprinting your style

People respond to gardens and spaces in different ways. A space is not necessarily filled with beautiful plants for you to think it pleasing or atmospheric, and sometimes the responses you have to particular places require some reflection. This is a less tangible aspect of garden assessment, but it is an essential part of the process of getting to know your garden. To a great extent such an analytical process says more about you as an individual and is often related to your life experiences.

A garden's atmosphere

Rather like when buying a new house, you are likely to experience a gut reaction to a garden when you first see it. There will almost certainly be something positive that you can identify within any space or garden that initially seems negative and miserable. Perhaps this might be relative to scale – a small and enclosed space might seem cosy to some and claustrophobic to others, overlooked by some and open and expansive to others.

The pattern of light and shade will often affect your understanding of the outdoor space. Dappled light sparkling through the light foliage canopy of birches can be a charming and endearing phenomenon, while the heavy permanent shade of a dominant beech or plane tree can create a sterile and miserable sense of permanent twilight.

Any negative response may be more to do with a lack of privacy, a feeling of discomfort with the layout or the sense of overdominant enclosure rather than a dislike of the plants contained within the garden.

It is important to identify and be aware of such responses, as they can affect whether you eventually change and develop the garden.

Exploitation of views

In urban areas, neighbouring or nearby buildings, with their blank or sterile blocks of hard materials, can often tower above a garden and block its views. Elsewhere views into adjacent gardens can soften vistas, and these can be exploited to develop a sense of greater space and depth. The Japanese call this technique the 'borrowed view'.

It is useful to assess and define the qualities of the views from your garden in order to take advantage of the best and to hide or disguise the worst. Evaluate views by considering the way in which sunlight and shadows fall, the activity observed during the day – a view of a street may not be considered beautiful but it will change dramatically and dynamically over time. Sometimes views can be better by night than by day, as street and floodlights take over from sunshine and daylight. Roof gardens in particular need to balance the exploitation of views with the protection of the garden from wind.

Coming to a decision

The evaluation of your garden in a dispassionate way can help you to come to some conclusions about what has value and should be retained and what needs to be removed. Sometimes such decisions are difficult and may need time for reflection and to make sure that you have come to the right design. At this early stage of planning it is useful to ask questions about even the most obvious garden features and to consider all options for change, because this can generate fresh thinking and new ideas.

Out with old, in with new

When weighing the benefits of existing features against your plans for the garden, you should bear in mind that the retention of established planting will give maturity to the garden even though it potentially also occupies precious space. Larger trees create scale and a shady atmosphere or dappled light, but they may be in awkward positions and could have outgrown the garden space. Some trees with larger leaves will produce excessive litter in the autumn, yet provide interest in other seasons.

In some well-established gardens extensive clearance is an essential part of moving on with your project. However it is easy to lose invaluable assets in the process, so bear in mind that new plants – unless purchased as mature specimens – will take time to reach the same level of maturity as existing larger shrubs and trees.

▶ **Painted render can introduce** strong pigments into the garden, and these can be repeated in flower and foliage colour. Gushing water adds drama and sound.

▶ ▶ **A Mediterranean atmosphere** has been evoked by the use of limestone and gravel planted with succulents and tender citrus trees found in such sunny regions.

Sculptural cubes of oak form stepping stones through the softer planting forms and textures in this deep border. The peeling bark of river birch (*Betula nigra*) repeats the colours of the timber.

Setting the agenda

When it comes to developing the design of your garden think carefully about how you want to use the garden. A productive garden will have a very different layout and character to one that is a relaxing retreat or a garden for entertaining friends.

List the features such as water, lighting or sculptures that you wish to include. Favourite colours, plants and materials can also make their way onto this wish list. Initially it can be wide-ranging, but eventually it should be reduced in scope.

Consulting others

When designing a garden it is helpful to visit other gardens to photograph planting and design ideas that appeal. Many small gardens open to the public from time to time, and these can provide useful food for thought as they reveal how other owners approach similar problems to your own. Keep a folder of images taken from books or magazines to help you focus on the character and atmosphere you seek.

Establishing priorities

The compilation of this wish list is fun and allows your imagination to fly. The hard work comes as you start to prioritize this information. The main restriction on the list is the limited size of your garden, and it is unrealistic to expect that everything to fit.

Simplify your thinking as much as possible, and place the main considerations in priority order. This reduction to the most important requirements simplifies the demands on the garden spaces and delivers a much more successful solution than ending up with a complex garden filled with many different features. The revised wish list can also help in identifying the cost of the proposed changes to the garden.

Planning your resources

The reality of garden-making is that it costs money. Quite how much depends on what you want to do and how you want to achieve it. If you are happy to clear away the old garden yourself and develop the new then you will save money. Approximately 30–50 percent of the cost of a garden is made up solely of labour charges if you choose to employ a contractor.

The DIY approach generally takes time as the work has to be done in your own leisure time. The main areas of hard work lie in clearance and the construction of paved areas and installation of special features such as lighting and water. You could always seek specialist help for these tasks, leaving the plant choice, sourcing and actual planting to be done by you.

◄ **Artificial grass is invaluable** in areas of extra-heavy wear, such as this play space. The area has been partially screened by hedges, which help to link the space with the rest of the family garden.

Can a designer help?

Employing a designer will add to the costs of creating a new garden. However a professional is likely to offer a wide range of ideas, which may lead to more imaginative solutions. They can support you through the construction and planting process, and sometimes they can save you money as they will advise against unnecessary expense.

If you plan to remain in your property for a long time then it is worth expending optimum thought, time and money initially so you can enjoy the garden to the full. Some garden owners stage the construction work in order to spread the costs.

▲ **Productive gardens, which** combine fruit, vegetables and flowers, need to be organized primarily as work spaces although they can be enjoyed visually too. Paths must be wide enough for wheelbarrows and should be paved for ease of use and maintenance. Vertical surfaces can also be put to good use.

Hardscaping costs

Hardscaping is always more expensive than planting. Although people would like their garden redesign to be cheap, the construction costs will be the equivalent or more than the costs of similar work in housebuilding. The quality of the materials also impinges on costs.

Slate, sandstone, limestone, basalt and granite are relatively expensive, while gravel is one of the cheapest materials available. Poured concrete with special finishes is high in cost, whereas precast concrete is relatively inexpensive. Brick paving combined with a trim of Yorkstone or slate of good quality should be available at a reasonable cost.

Plant costs

Planting can be expensive if you select mature and large-scale specimens, but costs can be reduced by purchasing smaller or younger plants.

Turf is one of the cheapest plant materials, but it is not always advisable to have a lawn in a small garden,

▲ **Garden furniture can take** up more space than you imagine, so you should make paved and functional areas as large as possible to allow for easy use.

especially if it is shaded. Plants grown from seed entail the lowest financial outlay but a high time investment and delayed maturity in your scheme.

A wildlife-friendly garden benefits from a sustainable or low-maintenance approach, here with informal, naturalistic planting and simple gravel paths.

BASICS:
CASE STUDY

A ROOFTOP RETREAT

This mature city roof garden, belonging to French designer Michèle Osborne, typifies the basic ways to make a successful garden in an exposed position.

Imaginative use has been made of this previously empty place by introducing a range of moods and atmospheres in a roof garden. The planting scheme had to take into account fixed structures such as access points, parapet walls and balustrades.

Such an exposed site also required shelter, as winds at this level can be destructive to most plants. Hedges and split bamboo screens help with this screening.

The old and the new

Existing features such as the utilitarian galvanized steel balustrade have been retained and painted in grey, while different surfaces are used for decorative planting, containers and incidental artefacts. The materials palette is restricted to a soft silver-grey in slate and weathered timber. Containers repeat this sense of control, although Michelle introduces a range of different forms and finishes.

At a lower level

A more intimate and shady courtyard provides a reflective and engaging space dominated by foliage textures. This space forms the entrance to the higher rooftop garden and is also viewed from the bedroom.

Design ideas to take home

- Use of a restricted palette of materials – wood and steel – gives a sense of unity.
- Repeat planting combinations retain simplicity and emphasize foliage textures.
- Shelter is provided from bamboo screens and hedges.
- Species have been chosen for hot and dry conditions.
- Generous spaces allow for entertaining and relaxation.

◀ **In the lower roof terrace** shade-tolerant plants have been mass-planted to soften the surroundings, while their richly patterned leaves offer a variety of textures. Ferns dominate the scene with hellebores providing seasonal interest and a changing backdrop to the bedroom alongside.

... a rooftop garden that celebrates sun, scent and sky...

CITY HIGH LIFE

A virtual hedge of lavender [1] bursts skywards on either side of the dining deck. Fragrant and colourful, it sets the tone in this sun-drenched space.

Behind is another hedge, this time of yew (*Taxus baccata*) [2], which forms a dense, dark backdrop to the lavender and shelters the garden from prevailing winds. The semipermeable bamboo screening [3] also helps in this respect.

More delicate plants such as purple buddleja [4] softened by transparent calamagrostis grasses flourish with this protection.

The entire garden planting is sustained in pots and planters in a range of styles from sophisticated zinc cubes to old galvanized barrels, and these give more permanent structure to the design, as do the box spheres and cones [5]. The consistent use of grey [6] unites the hard materials throughout.

Weight loadings are often a problem on roof gardens. Here lightweight timber decking [7] has been laid over a wide span to spread the load across the surface.

◀ **The mood in this garden** has been set by covering every available surface with a variety of plants. The cobbles and shingle on the flat roof provide a home for sedums and succulents in an eclectic range of pots.

SMALL GARDEN
DESIGN

As gardens get smaller the need for imaginative design becomes even more important. Spaces must work hard to accommodate different requirements and uses. Privacy has to be managed without creating heavily shaded, enclosed areas, and storage facilities have to be planned for.

In good garden design ideas, materials and layouts are simplified into a coherent plan. Imaginative solutions are found to seemingly intractable problems, and, if appropriate, bold colours, textures and unusual materials introduced for self-expression.

Investing time to design a small garden soon pays off, if it expands your living space and brings the experience of nature, space and light to your door.

15 ways to... make instant impact

1. Write a clear brief

Work to a clear brief that has been prepared and carefully considered before you start to tackle the garden. Changes of mind need to be kept to a minimum to avoid unnecessary spending and time wastage. The whole point of design is to plan first and then implement your ideas.

2. Know your dimensions

Check and draw out the dimensions of the garden in plan. This will enable you to see if the ideas you want to achieve and the elements you would like to include will all fit within the space. The more accurate this information is, the more successful your garden planning will be.

3. Identify key functions

Decide what you want to do in the garden. Some will view leisure and relaxation as important uses, and these will need a paved terrace for example. Others will want to devote as much garden as possible to planting; for this you need access paths and storage as well as the plants themselves.

4. Be lavish with space

Try to be as generous as possible with spaces in your layouts. Wider and larger paved areas conjure a feeling of spaciousness, while in simple, large planting areas you can layer plants into different heights and include larger plants that can screen and soften boundaries.

5. Don't skimp on paths

Paths should be a minimum of 1.2m (4ft) wide for general use, to allow two people to walk side by side. Remember that plants can often flop over the sides of borders to reduce path widths. Just because a garden is small does not mean that features have to be reduced in size – in fact the opposite is often true.

6. Allow room for dining

Decide how many people will be using the terrace if you want to eat alfresco. If you assume that a table for four is 1 x 1m (3 x 3ft), as a minimum you need to add 1m (3ft) to each dimension in order to have enough room for seating and general movement. This means that the smallest terrace should be 3 x 3m (10 x 10ft). This does not allow any space for outdoor cooking, so an area 4 x 4m (13 x 13ft) would be more successful and comfortable.

7. Consider all storage needs

Try to rationalize storage so that its impact on the garden is minimized and access to it is appropriate to the amount of use. Kitchen waste and other recycling are best sited close to the kitchen door, as you will need them regularly. Tool storage and garden compost may be better at the end of the garden or screened from view.

8. Big pots are better

Containers should be as large as possible to maximize the soil available for plant growth and water catchment. They can be fitted with individual reservoirs to aid watering and improve plant health.

9. Keep it simple...

Planting will always add complexity and richness to the garden so that ideas for layout and paving can be much more minimal and bold as a result. Your design should therefore be simple especially in terms of layout and organization.

10. ... and flexible

Try to ensure that your garden design is as adaptable as possible. Built-in furniture and barbecues can limit the way in which a space is used especially if you have different requirements at different times. Movable furniture and storage units can resolve this issue.

11. Think about light effects

Lighter-coloured paving materials such as limestone and sandstones will reflect light into small gardens and are especially useful in shade. They can also significantly increase

12. Be bold with sculpture

Ornament and sculpture should be bold and large in scale. If you feel that an artifact would sit well indoors then it will be too small in scale for use in the garden, especially if you want to have it as a focal point. Some smaller, more detailed elements may be invaluable alongside seats or dining areas in order to engage the eye at close quarters.

reflected light into interiors. Darker materials such as slate or basalt will absorb light while emphasizing the colour of foliage.

13. Install lighting

With ambient lights you can use the garden after dark, while spotlights can highlight specific features or focal points. Incorporate the lighting before the garden is constructed so that cable runs can be hidden.

14. Introduce water

Safety allowing, pools need to be large and deep because small bodies of water heat easily, creating conditions favourable to algal growth. Aeration through fountains or bubble jets can help to reduce temperatures and keep water fresh. Smaller fountains or features with tanks below ground also work well in restricted spaces.

15. Structures

Keep structures such as pergolas and arbours in scale especially if they are to support plants. A height of 2.1m (7ft) will give space for walking beneath without becoming entangled in climbers.

Great design opportunities

Space, or the lack of it, is ultimately the major limitation and challenge of the small garden. But this is likely to trigger clever solutions for storage, flexibility of use and planting in an imaginative design. Every square metre of space on the ground is valuable, and the exploitation of vertical surfaces and rooftops can also deliver surprising results.

Whether viewed as a whole or as a collection of confined spaces, small gardens play an important role in the exploitation and greening of towns and cities, offering diversity and protection to an extensive range of plant and animal species.

Planting opportunities

Despite often being heavily shaded, plant selection in a small garden can be charming and subtle. Shade planting generally relies for its impact on bold foliage texture and paler luminous flowers.

The introduction of screen planting, arbours and pergolas could be seen as clutter, yet the opportunity for more intimate and private spaces as a result is a considerable bonus. Shelter planting and screening for roof gardens also pay dividends, because they improve the microclimate and expand the range of plants that can be grown in such an exposed site.

What is certain with smaller spaces is that attention to detail really counts, as everything in the garden can be seen and explored at close quarters. Look at how materials and plants have been combined successfully in other gardens you visit.

Combined goal

The design process relies on assessing a range of alternative solutions and comparing the advantages and disadvantages of each approach, rather than taking *ad hoc* decisions based more on style or appearance. You are trying to combine your aspirations with functional requirements as well as to co-ordinate reflections of your personality, and that of your garden, with practical solutions. Your plan also needs to fit realistically within your garden space and be within an affordable budget.

Exploring all options

Your first design attempt may prove successful, but there is no reason to think that option one will be your best solution. Most designers produce two or three layouts and compare the merits of each, sometimes

◀ **Dense planting will screen** boundaries and create a perception that the garden is larger, especially if the planting is related to trees in the immediate surrounding landscape.

... in all small gardens, our attention to detail counts...

Why it works

The designer has prioritized space as a central, flexible feature. Expanses of concrete and timber deck provide visual interest and a surface. Planting is dense, tall and architectural, disguising boundaries. Flower colour picks up the tones of the timber and loungers in this lively, coherent design.

combining the best ideas from them. With this approach you can afford to be inventive, and you should try to overcome what may seem initially to be insurmountable problems.

Fine-tuning the plan

In a garden that includes a mature tree, for example, you might decide to retain the tree within design option one, but at least one of your other layouts should look at what happens to the garden if the tree is removed. The advantages of increased light and space or the ability to change garden levels may be outweighed by the loss of scale, character and habitat.

It is always worth exploring such issues on paper before the chain saw is sharpened. As a result of your experimentation you should be able to achieve the optimum garden design.

Decision time

Designing a garden around an existing tree that subsequently dies can be disheartening so always seek the advice of a professional about the health of the tree before including it in your final design.

Try to be pragmatic about existing features or plants that are not worth preserving, and meanwhile enjoy revealing hidden secrets or opening up new views.

▲ **Semi-open boundaries** such as palisade or hit-and-miss fences will reduce the impact of shade while retaining some degree of privacy.

The principles of design

When designing a small garden the principles of design become more important than in bigger spaces. Each of the principles in these pages will help you 'see' your garden from a new angle. Of overwhelming importance is a sense of clarity and simplicity in the development of your ideas.

Before you start to work with these principles it is worth asking a simple question. 'What is the big idea? 'When you think of a completed garden, what do you see in your mind and how would you best describe it?'

Finding a 'big idea'

Try to edit your thinking down into no more than three key descriptors. Words might help if you have difficulty in conceptualizing the 'big idea'.

Your 'big idea' for example might be framed as 'a secret retreat', suggesting an element of hidden solitude, separation or discovery. Key words that might deliver a similar goal could be 'quiet', 'haven' and 'private'.

Translating the idea

This concept suggests that planting might be used to soften the space and to introduce screening and separation. Reflective or lightly gurgling water might come to mind, as might dappled shade and tactile materials such as wood, which is warm to the touch. Darker surfaces might be suggested rather than brighter, reflective ones.

Flower colour might be soft or in the blue-purple spectrum, or white could offset green-textured foliage.

What is evident here is a train of thought that starts with abstract notions, then frames or describes an atmosphere, and finally suggests materials and perhaps a basic layout for the garden. Design principles support this approach and can be used to develop these ideas, organizing them into the optimum solution.

▶ **Maples, bamboo and hydrangeas** shield a quiet retreat at the end of this small garden as well as soften the surrounding boundary fence with their varied textures.

Soft tree ferns (*Dicksonia antarctica*) offer privacy and light shade in this enclosed urban garden with its simple planting palette of clipped box (*Buxus sempervirens*) and *Hakonechloa macra*.

A bold planting mass of taller shrubs and mature trees contrast effectively with the generous, brick-paved terrace set aside for relaxation.

Using layout & geometry

All gardens have some form of organized layout. In some it is very clear and legible, while in others the layout is more ambiguous. To understand a layout you should separate the planted elements from the geometry that controls the shape and size of terraces, paths, planting areas, storage facilities and water features.

Two-dimensional geometry can be organized into: squares and rectangles; circles and curved shapes such as ellipses; and triangles or angular shapes. Each of these shapes has a language of its own and also affects the mood in your garden and the way in which materials can be used. Geometry is therefore a fundamental design principle.

Scale and proportion are also important considerations when designing any layout. If possible make spaces more generous than the minimum you need. Check on the functional dimensions required to accommodate each shape in order to assess the proportions successfully.

Squares and rectangles

Of all the geometric shapes squares and rectangles are the easiest to fit together. Most paving materials are square or rectangular, which means that they easily follow rectilinear patterns, minimizing cutting, shaping and wastage, thereby reducing costs.

Squares are symmetric shapes providing a formal and equally balanced quality and a certain sense of formality or equilibrium.

Rectangles share many characteristics of squares, and they

▲ **Brick and stone paving** combine easily in a rectilinear design, echoed through the steps and retaining wall but softened by the mosses.

also introduce a sense of movement into the garden because they are longer in one direction, and the eye tends to follow the longer dimension.

Oblongs, which are elongated rectangles, emphasize this dynamic quality even more, and are often used for paths, rills or framed views.

Circles, curves and ellipses

Circles give a completely different character to the garden, because they have no corners to distract the eye. They offer a sense of uniformity and are what is known as self-centred shapes. In other words we tend to look for the middle of the circle. They are therefore a perfect shape to form the basis of a quiet retreat.

Unfortunately circles leave awkwardly angled shapes that are too narrow to be planted because they don't fit together neatly. Such visual tension points and acute angles can

be avoided by overlapping adjacent circles, opening up the junction to more of a right angle. For most people, circles are soft and fluid, but the appearance of sharp angles can be visually uncomfortable.

A paved circular shape generally has square or rectangular units laid across the circle, and these are shaped as they reach its edge. The units in a concentric paving pattern are reduced in size towards the centre as the pattern becomes tighter. Both these patterns take considerable time to lay, and so entail higher costs if done by a contractor.

It is possible to create a sense of direction or focus by using ellipses or ovals. These shapes retain their softer character, but their elongation creates a more dynamic sense of movement.

For curves in a path or lawn try to ensure the effect is smooth and fluid. Use a defined radius for your curves, and make sure path edges run parallel. If you draw out your curves on a plan with compasses, then the radius and radius point can be located and measured to repeat the pattern on the actual ground.

Triangles or angular shapes

Angular shapes can be the most difficult geometric element to use in a garden. They have a strong sense of direction, and their restless dynamic movement can distract the eye and sometimes tire the brain if the design is overcomplex.

The junctions and combinations in angular paving are suitable for complex patterns, into which offcuts can sometimes be incorporated. More complex shapes can be achieved using materials such as loose gravel or poured concrete, which can be made into any shape in its liquid state.

Creating unity

It is often desirable to retain a single geometric character throughout the garden as it simplifies the design. A layout with rectangular paving slabs for example laid in rectangular patterns within rectangular terraces and paths will have a satisfying sense of coherence and unity.

Curves and circular elements can be combined for a more dynamic quality. Aim to be bold and clear in your designs as planting will soften the edges of paved areas.

When circles are combined awkward angular junctions can arise. The closer the junctions are to a right angle the easier the junctions are to plant and soften.

◄ **Angles are the most dynamic** and lively elements to use, creating a visual tension that can be a dominant but restless force.

When you produce a drawing of your garden layout, it may be useful to shade or colour the main shapes so that you can read and balance the positive and negative elements together before the garden is built.

Optical tricks

If you wish to add a circular lawn to a garden 5m (16ft) wide the temptation is to make the lawn as large as possible, that is 5m (16ft) in diameter. This will spread the lawn to meet each side boundary, leaving no space for planting. In addition, the narrow and acute angles in the corners are virtually unplantable. However by introducing a border 1m (3ft) deep along each boundary, the remaining lawn becomes 3m (10ft) wide – much smaller than the original intention.

Using a technique known as subtractive geometry the eye can be deceived. It will read a shape even though the object can't be seen in its entirety. A square terrace with a small corner taken out for planting will still be interpreted and described as a square. Thus by moving the centre of the circular lawn away from the central axis of the garden it is possible to accommodate part of a circular lawn along with planted borders.

Ready-made solutions

Some paving manufacturers produce ready-made concentric paving that fits together neatly and is ideal for a small garden. Alternatively use smaller paving units such as setts or pebble mosaic. Gravel works with any shape or layout but needs a retaining edge.

▲ **Gravel and informal planting** softens the mixture of geometric forms and paving patterns here. The scene is balanced by lively planting textures.

Creating contrast

When planning your garden you may want to combine certain geometric shapes and materials for visual contrast. A circular deck or terrace overlapping a rectangular path or lawn will be eye-catchingly dynamic. Complexity also increases once planting is introduced so don't overwork the geometric ideas.

Positives and negatives

A circular lawn may be seen as a positive shape, but how can this best be fitted into a square or rectangular plot, which is the shape of most gardens? The leftover space is not designed in the same positive way – it is a negative space resulting from the addition of the lawn. In other words it is unlikely that you would design these shapes first, as they could be difficult to plant and manage, and be narrow and sharply pointed in places. Such negative shapes might well upset the visual balance of the garden.

This brick retaining wall with its
sweeping arc marks a level change
within the garden, while the rectangular
paving pattern enhances the simplicity
and coherence of the overall design.

Using space, volume & height

The framework that geometry provides is only one principle of garden design to control layout and horizontal dimensions. Because gardens are three-dimensional spaces it is also necessary to explore their height and volume.

Space and volume

Some gardens are small enough to be best used as a single space – in which case its three-dimensional elements are the boundaries and planting, with the possible addition of storage and containers. The main consideration here is that the addition of three-dimensional elements will occupy precious space, which if not carefully considered can feel drastically reduced and claustrophobic. This is a little like furnishing a room: it feels large when empty but may be cramped once the furniture is installed.

To minimize this psychological effect, introduce narrow tool storage cupboards along bare boundaries, instead of using a larger shed. One or two larger planting containers will have greater impact than a range of smaller pots, which will clutter the space. Another space-saving option is to have folding or movable tables, which can be withdrawn or reduced in size when not in use.

Slightly larger plots might benefit from the space being divided – with perhaps a dining area and a planting or productive area – to enhance the sense of depth and to add interest. They can be separated by constructed screens such as walls, fences or trellis, which occupy little floor space. Such features can be lit to reveal textures and surface patinas too.

Understanding 'height'

Using plants as building blocks as opposed to purely decorative elements is important spatially. Therefore when deciding on which plants to have in

Columns of hornbeam create additional height and planting mass here. By planting them into the lawn the border colour is playfully glimpsed and privacy is improved.

▲ **Cupboards for recycling** and tool storage are a necessary substitute for a shed in a smaller garden. They also provide additional surfaces for simple planting.

▶ **Bold, textured cylindrical** sculptures give height and vertical interest here, while the luxuriant planting and multistemmed trees provide compositional balance.

your new garden, always research the mature height and width of the species in which you are interested. Aim for variations in height.

Relate planting to your own height and eye level. Trees for example provide a good mass of foliage overhead, offering privacy and shade but enabling the space below to be utilized. Ground cover or knee-height planting allows the space above to be viewed, apparently increasing the size or depth of your garden.

Shrubs, perennials and grasses can form a loose or transparent barrier or screen, hinting at but not fully revealing what lies beyond. This can minimize shading within the garden, although taller shrubs will generally occupy more space than grasses and perennials.

Adding height by screening

Hedges take up more space and volume than a wall, fence or trellis, and this has important implications in a small garden. A typical hedge is around 1m (3ft) wide, whereas a wall averages 23cm (9in) wide and a trellis screen, supported by posts, is no wider than 10cm (4in).

A screen height of 1.8–2.1m (6–7ft) is required to enclose a space effectively, because those below eye level do not establish sufficient visual separation to encourage the curious to explore farther into the garden.

▶ **Hedges absorb sound** so are excellent as a backdrop to a quiet seating area – as here with yew (*Taxus baccata*). They also define spaces as well as block and control views.

Transparent woven hurdles are spatially efficient dividers. Here they define a sheltered and intimate courtyard space in which tender and exotic *Brugmansia* x *candida* 'Grand Marnier' is displayed.

Disguising your boundaries

Although your garden will have some form of boundary its type, height and quality will vary. In older gardens there may be characterful brick or stone walls, while in new-build properties the boundary may be low, lightweight fencing panels (see pp116–117).

How to disguise a boundary

If for convenience you decide to retain your existing boundary as an integral part of your new design, you can still make it look different by concealing it with vegetation. Plants such as climbers or wall shrubs, taller grasses and bamboos can screen untidy combinations of materials in the boundary or even disguise the actual location and form of the boundary itself. By introducing a sense of ambiguity the actual extent and size of the garden can be visually fudged.

Climbers occupy the least space when mature, while shrubs or taller perennials and grasses develop greater volume and have a more three-dimensional effect, allowing highlights and shadows to break up the line of the boundary. Climbers make useful backdrops to such planting schemes.

BOUNDARY DISTRACTIONS

1. **Hazel or willow branches** can be woven into simple hurdles – ideal for rural locations or for private spaces in communal gardens.

2. **Hedging such as box** works well as a planted boundary and to disguise walls or fences that you may be unable to remove.

3. **Open trellis work** and fence panels are sympathetic surfaces for climbers. Steel vine eyes can also be used for support if necessary.

4. **Openings and windows** can be built into walls, to take advantage of special views. Here a bench, shaped to the window detail, has been positioned in front of the wall.

5. **Climbers can soften the** appearance of boundaries and add visual interest. Here *Parthenocissus tricuspidata* shows its autumn colours against a silvered close-board fence.

Allow planting to break into the main garden space, perhaps as an alternative to a lawn. Deeper borders of around 1.5m (5ft) in depth will allow layered planting and a variety of heights.

Marking out your borders

A small garden often has a central usable space and planting beds scattered around the outer edges. These borders are too narrow to be effective as visual features or for plant health. It is also difficult for plants to grow in such borders, at the base of a boundary or house wall, where they suffer from drought because walls and foundations can absorb moisture from the soil. In addition plants are affected by rain shadow, which means that rain blown by the wind rarely falls in the shelter of a taller wall.

For these reasons plants need to be placed at least 45cm (18in) away from any wall, and so any border against a boundary must be more than this measurement in depth.

Maximize planting impact

A border should be designed to take plant growth into account. For example a small shrub may grow to an eventual spread of 1m (3ft). Borders of 1m (3ft) depth will therefore house one shrub depth and have little space left for anything else. The possibility of including visual interest or screening is therefore limited. Smaller perennials may prove more

successful, but their scale will have a reduced impact on the garden.

Borders 1.5m (5ft) or more deep allow plants to be layered both in their heights and in their depth and positioning within the border. Shrubs, perennials and grasses may look eye-catching when planted side by side, or just perennials of different heights and forms could be selected.

Thus by reviewing different garden layouts it may prove that a single large border, with its greater mass of planting to balance non-planted areas, will work better than a series of smaller borders along every boundary.

Understanding 'void' & 'mass'

The sense of three-dimensional balance within a garden is best summarized as a satisfying combination of solids (the mass) and space (the void). Solid mass refers to planting, even though structures such as sheds or summerhouses are also 'solid'. Planting however has a softening impact on the garden as well as forming a three-dimensional mass.

▲ **Design with** approximately 10 percent mass and 90 percent void.

Finding a happy balance

A completely empty garden will be 100 percent void and a complete jungle would be 100 percent mass. Neither extreme is entirely comfortable or suitable for our needs. Ideally a relationship of 25–50 percent mass and 75–50 percent void would create usable space and has visual appeal. Lawns would count as void in this assessment because it is usable open space. It is worth exploring this method of judging the success of other gardens before planning your own.

▲ **Design with** approximately 40 percent mass and 60 percent void.

DIY DESIGN

A trick for the eye

- Even in small spaces it is possible to trick the eye with a false or artificially exaggerated perspective.
- In perspective, objects appear to get smaller the farther away they are. Paths or lawns can be narrowed at the far end to create a false sense of distance.
- Plant specimens of the same type, of diminishing sizes, along the length of the path or lawn, and gradually reduce the distances between the plants.
- Enhance the effect by planting finer-leaved species toward the rear of the garden and larger-leaved ones closer to the house.
- All design tricks work only from a fixed viewing position (see also pp50–51).

With its open lawn this garden has
a fairly high percentage of void in its
design. This is tempered by the generous
depth and mix of planting.

For a high percentage of mass make
borders as large as possible, so a range
of plant sizes can offer plenty of layered
screening and textural variation.

Saving space through design

More than anything, design is a problem-solving process that needs to marry function and appearance with a coherent goal. With small gardens the main concern is how to match their limited space with the perceived needs for that area, which may well be overambitious and unrealistic.

Tackling the wish list

Many people compile a wish list of ingredients for their ideal garden, without giving much thought as to how much space each element will occupy. They may for example want dining, play, relaxation, storage and compost areas as well as a vegetable garden.

An initial reaction to such a long list of needs might be to allocate everything – or almost everything – a small space side by side. However this often overcrowds the garden and creates a series of miniature and often unworkable features that together increase complexity and difficulty in

use. Paths become too narrow to use (a minimum width should be 1.2m/4ft) or furniture proves too big for the designated terrace (at least 1m/3ft is required on each side of a garden table for chairs and access). Where

▲ **For a versatile surface** in a small family garden introduce decking, which can hide a range of storage or children's play options.

space has become limited, planting is often reduced in scale and impact.

DIY DESIGN

Tree seats for form and function

- Tree seats provide a wonderful focal point in the garden and can revitalize an old tree as a new feature.
- Such seats are best installed around a mature specimen, as the trunk will give better scale and a backdrop to the seating area.
- Allow space for the trunk to broaden with age by ensuring that the seat is not fixed too tightly around the trunk; also the tree seat should be freestanding and not attached to the tree.
- Take care that fixings and foundations for permanent seats do not interfere with existing roots. Some tree species root extremely close to the surface and can easily be damaged.

Doubling the benefits

Alternatively each element you consider for the garden needs to multitask. Seats can double up for storage, tables fold or slide to reveal a more versatile paved surface, and (as illustrated left), play features such as sandpits can be dropped below decks. Movable planters can be repositioned within the garden, according to the seasons, and thus the whole garden space can be reconfigured strikingly.

Vertical areas

By making maximum use of vertical and horizontal surfaces for storage, pressure is taken off limited floor space in a small garden.

Vertical planting takes this concept further and removes traditional flowerbeds from the precious and more usable horizontal surfaces, simplifying the design of small gardens in one move. This can result in greater diversity of planting as well as spaces that are greener than the often limited planting space left over once other functional needs have been accommodated.

With vertical planting systems, the plants are accommodated in small pockets that can easily dry out. Therefore such systems need to include watering systems to keep the plants moist and growing heathily. Planting can be selected to cope with shaded locations as well as for full sun. These vertical systems are also usable for fruit, vegetables and herbs.

Optimum space dividers

Walls occupy less space than hedges, while fences or trellis will take up even less space. If you want a softer character to your garden, plant climbers to 'green' its hard elements.

Trees require little floor space, while their light-filtering or transparent canopies bear a mass of foliage at high

▲ **These lightweight, individual benches** are ideal for flexible seating. They are decorative when not in use and add eye-catching colour.

level, which offers privacy for garden users, nesting opportunities for birds and shelter from the wind as well as visual drama – a bold response to a spatial dilemma.

The ancient art of pleaching, in which hedges are stilted on clear stems, also creates space beneath for additional planting.

Planting roofs

Green roof systems are becoming increasingly popular and provide planting opportunities and visual interest in spaces that would be otherwise sterile and unused (see p142). For example the tops of storage cupboards can be planted with simple herbs or salads to optimize available surfaces (see p40). Be inventive in the way you utilize such spaces.

Adding design tricks & treats

Playful tricks can resolve and sometimes transform small spaces, deceiving the eye and the brain into reading a larger garden. The art of such deception lies in the detail.

Trompe l'oeil

Trompe l'oeil is a deception provided by painted imagery often applied to a smooth, rendered surface. Typically views, false windows, steps and paths create the illusion of space beyond the boundary walls. When used in combination with planting that softens or hides the edges of the painted wall these deceits can be highly effective.

Ideally they should be viewed from an identifiable vantage point, as the perspective in the images will distort as you move around the garden.

Reflective surfaces

Mirrors or mirrored surfaces have frequently been introduced in order to expand the visual sense of space in a small urban garden, and when cleverly positioned they are indeed convincing. Unfortunately birds can injure themselves on large expanses of mirror because they also are taken in by the deceit. By positioning transparent plants such as ornamental grasses in front of the mirror you reduce the danger for birds.

The best results are obtained from mirrors that drop down to ground level from the top of your boundary walls, as they reflect the ground and continue the illusion of a space beyond. Always keep mirrored surfaces clean and ensure that the framing is not too obvious. Ideally plants that surround the mirror can diffuse its edges.

Perspex, stainless steel and some ceramic surfaces can be placed to reflect light rather than to be perfect mirrors. The resulting light effects can lift the mood and will change as sunlight levels vary across the day.

Playing with perspective

Experimenting with the rules of perspective can enhance a sense of depth, especially in a long, narrow

◀ **Mirrors conjure spectacular effects** and play visual tricks, but they can also be hazardous for birds. Use them in association with planting to reduce the danger.

▲ **Here polished stainless steel** reflects an ever-changing light, while a thin film of bird-friendly water breaks up the dynamic surface in this slate wall.

garden. The parallel lines of a path for example will appear to converge over distance as you look along its length. By laying a path that is wider close to your viewing position and narrower at its farthest point, perspective will be exaggerated and your space will seem longer. Continue the deception in the planting alongside with bold foliage and taller plants close by and finer foliage textures and smaller plants at the end of the path. As with *trompe l'oeil*, however, this trick will work from only one main vantage point, and as you move around the garden the angled lines can seem awkward.

A route full of surprises

- Design an indirect path or a series of interlocking paved areas to establish either a meandering route or a series of corners and changes of direction. This will enable users to enjoy a variety of different views.
- Set plants such as a hedge alongside a path. It should be tall enough to block views through the garden. Taller shrubs and perennials can also be planted for a softer or more natural effect. Trellis panels for climbers may also be included where space is limited.
- Introduce a strategically placed ornament or sculpture to distract the eye while you are walking along the route. This is especially effective when sited where the path changes direction.

Using colour in your garden

When designing your planting scheme it is important to remember that flower colour is much more transitory than foliage colour, although the lure of the livelier flower colour ranges is always tempting. Therefore variations in the leaf and stem colours should be considered too.

Colour combinations

The successful exploitation of colour relies more on how colours are brought together than on any individual colour. For example if you wish to use red then choose from a selection of colours in the red spectrum. Red used with red-purple and purple-red will offer a sensation of red while the various hues will provide greater depth to the planting.

High colour contrast contributes to lively planting, yet the eye and brain can quickly tire. Therefore if you have a small space it may be more relaxing to reduce (but not completely remove) contrast. The highest differences are between the primary colours – red, blue and yellow – and between primaries and secondary colours (which are also known as complementaries). Reds are complemented by greens; blues by oranges; and yellows by purples.

Colour perceptions

Consider how you will view these colours. Red for example will seem more obvious and larger against a black backdrop than against a white one, whereas yellow will seem more luminous and larger against a white backdrop than against a black one.

The massing of colour by using blocks or larger drifts of a single species will emphasize and strengthen the effect, enabling the flower hues to compete with solid blocks of painted or material colour used for backdrops and boundaries. Colour massed in this way always produces greater impact than individual spots of colour.

Colour and light

Colour relies on light for its impact. Look at how sunlight works within

▼ **Bold orange perennials** are somewhat muted by the colouring in the busy dry-stone wall, whereas the green foliage stands out against its black backdrop.

▶ **A jungle of foliage** can prove just as eye-catching as a mass of flowers. Here rusted canna leaves, hemerocallis spears and leathery eriobotrya jostle for attention.

your garden and plan colours accordingly. Shade restricts flower colour especially, yet white flowers and foliage tend to work well here, often creating luminous effects.

Colour for emphasis

Darker paving colours such as slate, engineering brick, basalt or darker concrete lend emphasis to green foliage because they absorb more light. Many of these materials darken when wet, altering the atmosphere and sometimes reflecting surrounding colours in the glistening surface. Adjacent colours are often intensified.

Light materials such as limestone and pale sandstones reflect more light and create a livelier atmosphere, but this can sometimes reduce the impact of adjacent colour. Therefore select stronger-hued flower colours when planting alongside pale paving.

If foliage rather than flowers is to dominate your planting scheme it can be accompanied by intense, manufactured colours such as the dense orange-brown of corten weathering steel, the brilliant hues of ceramics, coated steels, paints or textiles. When concentrating on flower colour, ensure that it can compete with the solid blocks of colour alongside.

Coloured walls and fences

Think carefully before painting walls and fences around the garden as this will present an ongoing maintenance task. Timber is best stained as the colour is absorbed into the material rather than remaining on the surface.

▲ **The dense purple** base colouring of *Aster* 'Little Carlow' is intensified by the tiny jewellike flowers of *Verbena bonariensis*, which burst and float in the air.

▲ **Optimizing the autumn sunlight** is *Deschampsia cespitosa* 'Goldschleier', which glows in a haze of dried seedheads and echoes the rust-brown corten steel wall.

Using texture in your garden

Plant textures vary in form and quality, and the individual character of plant parts such as leaves can be feathery or solid, veined or smooth. Branches and stems or trunks also have textured surfaces with peeling or fissured bark, polished or hairy twigs. In addition leaves are arranged in particular patterns, thereby enhancing their foliage texture. By using these different aspects offered by plants, you can compose planting schemes and organize textures in the same way as you would colour (see p52).

Exploiting textural variation

Textural contrast always adds visual excitement and pleasure to the garden, and yet it is frequently overlooked in garden composition. People often shy away from bold foliage as perhaps they might from strident colour, but if all textures within a garden are too similar the result will be bland.

Plant textures are also more obvious when plants are organized into groups or masses of the same species. A group of fine grasses such as *Stipa tenuissima* emerging from the low, glossy mounds of bergenia foliage will work more successfully than one specimen of each species standing side by side.

Think also of the form of plants with vertical emphasis, such as irises, contrasted with mounded forms, such as clipped box (*Buxus*). Visit other gardens to identify successful textural associations and record or assess the proportion of each species used.

Leaf textures

A hedge is often positioned as a textured backdrop to planting. Often it is of a species bearing small leaves, needles or scales with dense branching that responds well to regular pruning and trimming. This is one reason why many conifers are chosen for hedging. For example yew (*Taxus baccata*) develops into a dark green, finely textured hedge. Box or Portuguese laurel (*Prunus lusitanica*) produces a dense hedge too but with a greater degree of texture as the leaves are larger than yew's needles.

Deciduous species are often termed broadleaved because their foliage is larger in scale than that of conifers and most other evergreens. Trees such as hornbeam (*Carpinus*) or beech (*Fagus*) with their ribbed and glossy leaves are more obviously textured. Both trees retain their foliage into winter, when it is copper coloured.

Evergreen climbers such as *Clematis armandii*, trachelospermum or ivy (*Hedera*) will provide a year-round textural backdrop to rival any hedge, producing smooth and dark, glossy leaves. Deciduous climbers bear a more dynamic range of colour across the seasons, and this variety rivals that of their wide textural range.

Composing with texture

When designing with texture consider the overall form of the plants you select. Some will be tall and erect, some arching and some low and spreading. Organize or group these forms or species so that the same or similar textures can be read as structured masses or drifts. This will provide a more unified composition than a whole series of different textures randomly arranged.

Use ornamental grasses for transparency and to bring light and movement into your planting groups. These species allow textures to be layered and develop a sense of depth in your planting. Light penetrating into the borders will also reveal different textural compositions as the sun

◀ **Mass planted** *Stipa tenuissima* with its delicate, feathery transparency complements the solidity of a stone sphere in this simple planting combination.

moves across the space, enhancing highlights and deep shadows.

Look at similarities and differences between the plants that you are considering for your scheme. Leaves of two unrelated species may have a similar shape, but one may be dark and glossy, the other pale and soft or unreflective. Combine plants that share some similarities but provide a sense of contrast too.

Think about how plant stems and branches create patterns and repetition. This also produces textural

interest in all seasons but is perhaps especially noticeable in winter as deciduous foliage disappears.

Texture from materials

The surfaces of paving and building materials provide a range of textures, both inherent to the material and derived from the way they are used. Light and shadow play can reveal the jointing patterns in walls and paving so they have a substantial impact. More minimalist schemes will use smooth

▲ Textural interest can be extended by growing plants in containers. Water plants also offer a good range of leaf variations.

surfaces, and joints will be minimized and mortar colour-matched.

Texture can be emphasized not only by sunlight but also by artificial light after dark, transforming the mood in the area. To draw attention to textures and patterns, position uplighters at the bases of walls. Low-level lights can similarly pick up the surfaces of terraces and paths.

Keep circular features large and as sharply defined as possible so that junctions are less acute. Even partial circles are legible and visually understood.

How to apply the principles

Small gardens come in all sorts of different shapes and sizes, and general design principles have to be adapted to suit these various challenges, such as the height at which the garden is sited.

Roof gardens

Gardens on the tops of buildings present specific challenges, because their layouts are governed by the supporting structures of the buildings on which they sit. Weight loading is an important consideration, and it is essential to consult a structural engineer about your plans, especially if you are considering converting an existing flat roof into a garden.

Balconies are in effect small roof gardens, and many of the same considerations need to be met.

Soil and paving on roofs

Soil is a heavy material but when wet its weight increases tremendously. Lawns require a 15–20cm (6–8in) soil depth; smaller shrubs, grasses and perennials need a soil depth of 30–45cm (12–18in), while larger shrubs require 50–100cm (1½–3ft) depth and trees 1–1.5m (3–5ft). Soilless potting composts are lighter in weight than soil-based ones. Even so, all weight implications need to be assessed when planting a roof garden.

In some modern developments these planting depths can be dropped

▶ **Plants in most roof gardens** have to be pot-grown in soilless compost. They should be carefully placed according to weight loading.

into the roof space below so the planting is at the same level as the paving. In most cases the planting is either in containers that are built into the fabric of the roof or in movable pots on the roof surface. Larger containers can be part-filled with lightweight non-soil fillers to reduce weight loading, although this will also reduce soil depths.

Paving can be lifted slightly above roof level by using spacers. This not only avoids the use of mortar and solid paving bases, which can add weight to the garden, but also more importantly it allows the roof to drain freely below

▼ **Even the tiniest roof** spaces and balconies can prove to be invaluable oases in which practicality and pleasure are combined.

◀ **Entrances are generally** enhanced by the careful positioning of plants. If containerized, the planting can be changed seasonally for different moods.

inadvertently bring the paving or soil into contact with a neighbour's wall above the level of its damp course. This could cause damp problems in the neighbour's property.

Basement screens

Try to include structures such as pergolas and arbours if you have the space. These need not be planted but can lend a sense of privacy to a basement garden.

Front gardens

Gardens that create entrances or might be located to the front of your property have a different role to those at the rear of the property, which are often more private. Such gardens are about making a good first impression and will often focus on a path. Design the path so that visitors do not have to walk in single file and allow as much space as possible by the front door.

Lighting is useful here but it is important not to be too ostentatious. Front gardens are the least secure of all garden spaces so think twice before placing valuable objects or ornaments there. Also check out the character of the local area and how your neighbours use materials and planting. There is room for individuality, but a sense of context is an important aspect of your design.

Legislation in some countries requires that front gardens are permeable, allowing rainwater to either pass through to the ground or to be collected within the garden in soakaways or drainage systems rather than spilling onto the public highway.

paving level. This in turn ensures that the roof remains waterproof.

Protecting roof gardens

Semi-open screens such as trellis or slatted fences that provide windbreaks will slow the wind speed and reduce its impact on the plants and garden users. Safety is also essential for balustrades, which should be at least 1.1m (3¹⁄₂ft) in height above the paved level of the garden.

Basement gardens

Basements are some of the most overlooked urban spaces, so privacy and shade are the major challenge here. More light can be reflected into the garden by pale-coloured walls and

paving materials, while darker colours can make the garden feel larger. Planting is often better viewed against darker backgrounds.

Colours in the red spectrum engender a tangible sense of warmth but will make the space feel smaller, whereas colours from the blue spectrum generally look cooler and make the space apparently larger.

If shade is particularly heavy in a basement garden, give emphasis to foliage textures and patterns rather than to planting colour or plants intended to provide fragrance.

Paving and soil in such areas must always be kept at ground level when adjacent to boundaries, which frequently will be the walls of neighbouring houses. This restriction is because you might otherwise

Soft tree fern (*Dicksonia antarctica*) softens this scene of cascading water. Its delicate, transparent fronds lean out across the pool.

SCREENING THE VIEWS

This garden by designer Andrew Wilson is a good example of how a small suburban garden that is overlooked on every side can be transformed into a haven of privacy.

Yew (*Taxus baccata*) hedges, which run across the garden, break up the space and reduce the visual impact of the boundaries. Each subdivision contains plants of a different group or association. Seasonal emphasis changes around the garden from early spring highlights through summer and autumn to winter-interest areas. The planting beds are in elegant curves and ellipses.

The green foliage tones of the plants are enhanced by the dark-coloured basalt chippings in the paths, which have been edged with steel to keep their shape and precision.

Although privacy is important in this garden, the end of the garden has been left open so the vegetable area at the end of the gravel path receives the full benefit of the sun.

The fences and trellis cladding have been stained black to reduce their dominance, while climbers soften their appearance further.

▲ **Tightly clipped yew hedges** divide the garden into seasonal planting areas. In this late-summer border the dark basalt gravel is washed with a wave of flowers and foliage of pheasant's tail grass (*Anemanthele lessoniana*).

Terrace privacy

To shield the main terrace by the house from external gaze, towering, transparent reeds have been planted in the adjacent pool. Their foliage allows light to penetrate, yet it also screens the seating area. The use of such large-scale planting within a smaller garden is important, because it maintains much-needed drama and visual interest.

The pool water is filtered through the reed bed to maintain its clarity and is planted with scented waterlilies. Reflections in the pool are matched by those on the black basalt terrace, which glimmers when wet.

Design ideas to take home

- Hedges have been used to divide the space and create an illusion of greater size.
- Separate planting areas create greater variety and a sense of discovery.
- Bold specimen plants give a feeling of scale and height to the garden.
- Dark paving (basalt) contrasts with the foliage and colour planting.
- Paving is reflective when wet and paler when dry, to change the mood.
- Steel-edged beds and paths establish a sense of order and definition and contrast with the softer drifts of perennials and grasses.
- Tall but transparent reeds shield the main seating area because the garden is overlooked.
- The borders are as deep as possible to maximize planting impact. Here they break into the lawn to provide screening and visual interest.

… rich contrasts of light and shade bring the garden to life…

MIRRORED IMAGES

Tall, elegant but transparent reeds (*Schoenoplectus lacustris* subsp. *tabernaemontani*) [1] are planted into the gravel-filled filter bed for the pool, creating dramatic reflections of light and shade in the water. They also offer privacy from overlooking properties.

On the far side of the pool a perennial and grass border [2], with its summer colour and hazy reflections, sweeps majestically around the lawn.

Scented waterlilies (*Nymphaea*) [3] float across the still, glassy water and perfume the evening air for those sitting on the terrace.

SMALL
GARDEN

STYLES

Style and design are often confused. Design is a process through which a wide range of issues will be resolved, while style relates to the way that the design solution is delivered. Particular colours, shapes or materials might combine into a style, and the way those elements are arranged can express stylistic ideas.

Style may reflect particular historical periods or movements in art such as classical or Modernism. Some garden styles are defined more by their function – for example vegetable gardens.

The age or architecture of your property could impact on your thinking, while styles can affect your choice of materials and garden plants.

15 ways to... find your style

1. Do the research

Clarify the style that you might want to use in the garden by fully researching the period, its materials and garden designers. This will inform you of layout, proportion and scale. Formal gardens relate loosely to the classical garden but can be interpreted in many ways. Other styles such as Art Nouveau are specific in their layout, colour combinations and range of typical materials.

2. Visit gardens

Go to as many gardens as possible that exemplify your preferred style. Nuances and idiosyncrasies in each will show how designs vary within a given designation, allowing the designer's personality and individuality to surface.

3. Exploring a culture

Some styles are based on cultural and philosophical approaches to garden-making, and it is worth exploring and understanding the background to these gardens. Many types of garden in Japan are often interpreted in an overgeneralized way, combining ornamentation from across the entire range.

4. Consider fusion

Recently there has been a trend to fuse or combine stylistic approaches, sometimes referred to as fusionism or historically as eclecticism. Here the best or strongest elements from different styles are combined. However take care not to overdo the approach, because too many different references can result in confusion or chaos. Aim for some coherence – perhaps through colour or repeated planting.

5. Complement architecture

The architectural style of your home will dominate your garden through its window or door treatments and the materials used in construction. Edwardian building is typically brick, although some used ornate terracotta tiling. Contemporary architecture uses timber cladding, steel and expanses of glass.

6. Look at furniture

Include garden furniture in your stylistic approach. Modern resin furniture would be incongruous in an Arts and Crafts garden, while a bench inspired by Sir Edwin Lutyens would be out of place in a Modernist space.

7. Pinpoint key descriptors

Once you have identified a style, isolate the key elements that define it. This may relate to overall layout, spatial composition, materials and typical plant species and forms. Colour might also typify certain styles: for example white is often associated with Modernism and richer earth tones with Mediterranean-style gardens.

9. Visit garden shows

Often designers explore stylistic ideas when they produce exhibits for garden shows, such as this one for the Chelsea Flower Show. The gardens are often accurate reproductions or inspired by particular styles. It is useful to see these new adaptations of garden styles and to be able to talk to the designer about the process.

10. Maintain scale

Look at the size and proportion of the main elements in your chosen style. A common mistake is to downsize these so that everything becomes smaller and the whole garden overcomplex.

8. Be original

Invest in some element of craftsmanship or art. The inclusion of an interesting and appropriate sculpture, ornament or something more structural, such as this retaining wall made from layers of stone, can help in setting the scene and emphasizing your style.

11. Consider the climate

When selecting species for more exotic styles such as Mediterranean or subtropical gardens ensure that they are appropriate to your climate. Urban centres form heat islands, which can moderate temperatures upward by three or four degrees Celsius, allowing less hardy plants to survive colder winters in cool-temperate climates. Suburban and rural gardens are prone to more severe frosts and have completely different microclimates.

12. Match plant styles

Planting selection should be true to style especially for key species, such as yew hedging for an English flower garden or olives for a Mediterranean atmosphere. There is no need to be pedantic about this process though – most modern cultivars represent an improvement on older varieties.

13. Assess maintenance

Be realistic about the work involved in maintaining a particular garden style.

14. Have an eye for detail

Once the overall structure of the garden is settled, consider the elements of detail that will add interest and authenticity to the design. Containers, furniture, lighting and sculpture can help to ensure that the garden makes a more convincing impact. Architectural salvage yards are fascinating hunting grounds for artifacts and desirable objects that convey a specific period or style.

In general greater variety in planting involves more time in maintenance. Water features require upkeep, and vegetable gardens especially need a dedicated time commitment.

15. Reinterpret the style

Accept that your garden may not be the same size as those that inspire you, so do not try to adopt any style too rigidly. The important thing is to prioritize the bits that will work – perhaps the colour and texture of hard materials or the repetition of key plant species.

Finding a style of your own

Styles help to organize and structure your garden, providing guiding principles and a coherent framework. This range of styles will help you select what feels right for you and suits your personality. The order and symmetry of the formal is contrasted with the unruly diversity of the cottage garden.

The formal approach

This is one of the most popular approaches to garden-making, and it is based on classical influence and symmetrical order. In some ways it is an easy style to adopt because it has clear rules that have been successfully repeated throughout the history of garden-making.

Connections can be traced through the classical gardens of Europe to the paradise gardens of Islam and the Mogul empire. Ancient formal gardens followed the quadripartite system based on the four rivers identified in the Garden of Eden. Using lawns, paving, water and hedges or controlled woodland as key materials, the classical gardens of Italy and France employ this system and set incredible geometric patterns within the landscape. They are often seen as expressions of power over nature.

Although modern formal gardens have adapted these original concepts, those of axial control, symmetry and repetition remain central.

Formality in a small garden

In a small garden expressions of power and dominance are generally impossible and probably undesirable, but the ability to divide even a tiny space into equal parts around a central axis is entirely workable.

A central axis or view is a good place to start, but it needs a focal point. This could be a seat or piece of sculpture. The simplest shapes to use are squares or preferably rectangles, which combine easily. Rectangles or oblongs give a sense of movement through their longer dimensions. Rectangular borders on either side of the path are normally edged with clipped hedges, often box (*Buxus sempervirens*), to create the order and precision needed (see also p174).

It is essential to retain a good sense of scale and proportion by keeping the layout simple. This will produce larger areas of planting or paving and allow for generous paths.

Dividing into four parts

If space permits, a cross axis can be introduced, thus producing four separate planting beds. In this scenario the focal point is often located at the intersection of the paths. Seats placed at the end of the paths can also act as focal points as well as offer views across the garden.

Think also about the functional needs you have in the garden, which

Clipped box hedges such as these in designer Isabelle Van Groeningen's garden at RHS Chelsea Flower Show give definition and clarity to planting.

7 ways to create a formal garden

- Retain a sense of simplicity in your pattern-making in order to maximize planting areas and space for paths of a generous width.
- Use low hedges to give clear definition to your planted areas.
- Introduce specimen plants or clipped ones to add height to the garden. Obelisks or frames for climbing plants can also assist this.
- Keep paving simple, although it can include a different edging material to enhance the geometric pattern. Loose gravel with formal edging in stone or steel can work well as a neutral but low-cost option.
- Water needs to be reflective if used as a pool, while fountains and spouts produce sound and movement. Smaller water features such as wall fountains or basins can become focal points. Water planting is either absent or carefully controlled to retain the formality.
- Establish symmetry as much as possible as this introduces the necessary repetition and order to a formal garden.
- Repeat key plants or associations in the planting. This can be informal if edged with low hedging. Vegetable gardens work well in a formal garden because of the ordered rows and repetition.

Key garden designers using a formal style: Arabella Lennox-Boyd, George Carter, Luciano Giubbilei

▲ **Formal layouts can** be traced back through history to ancient Moorish gardens such as those at the Alhambra and to the classical gardens of Europe.

▲ **Themes and layouts** often remain similar in formal gardens, which make use of axial organization and repeated arches. Focal points and features are also important.

an imposed formal layout can sometimes override.

The relatively narrow paths that result from a small garden being subdivided into four should be paved,

because grass will suffer from too much concentrated wear.

In an irregularly shaped plot, impose the design and allow the layout pattern to run out into the boundaries.

◀ **Zinc rectangular wall panels** and an oblong water tank set the mood here. The organic forms of cloud-clipped hornbeam and dense ground cover soften the hardscaping.

Perpendicular counterpoint

Vertical emphasis with its strong perpendiculars is an essential aspect of Modernist design. Some plants such as cypress, *Juniperus scopulorum* 'Skyrocket' and *Calamagrostis* x *acutiflora* 'Karl Foerster' are therefore more appropriate than others such as Mexican orange blossom (*Choisya*), which is more rounded and blobby.

The Modernist style developed from the Bauhaus School in Germany in the early 20th century, as a response to the new world of manufacturing and mass production. Man-made materials such as concrete, steel and glass are typical. Along with its clearly defined geometry these key elements are still evident in much of contemporary garden design. Decorative detail and ornamentation are significantly reduced or removed entirely, so that surfaces act as flat planes to reflect light or patterns of dappled shade.

The basic layout

Rectangles and squares form the basic layout in the garden and are overlapped asymmetrically. Paths can be represented by simple rectangles of paving, for an informal arrangement of spaces through which you can walk. Spheres or cubes of topiary are chosen for their pure, geometric form.

Planting should be designed for foliage interest and contrasts as much as for colour. It tends to be in large blocks or masses with specimen plants or clipped hedges introduced for emphasis (see p176).

Patterns are limited to simple rectilinear ones and joints are narrow. Thus, favoured paving materials are smooth-finished concrete (often poured *in situ*) or natural stone. Walls

The Modernist approach

Modernism shares certain attributes with the formal or classical approach (see p66). Geometry is clearly emphasized and legible with sharply defined lines, and key elements are often repeated for impact. However asymmetry pervades this style, so it has a much more dynamic and unpredictable character. For some people, this expresses a sense of freedom; for others, disorder.

The important element in Modernism is space and the way in which light and shadow interact. There is no exact formula involved, but areas of open space should balance with textured or taller planted areas. Hedges or walls are used as screens so they partially divide different parts of the garden. As these elements do not fully enclose a space, both light and air can flow from one part to another.

▲ **The planting here looks** sculptural, softening rectilinear elements and the clear-cut geometry of paving, water and surfaces.

7 ways to create a Modernist garden

- Use simple and clearly defined geometry for paved and planted areas. Rectangles and squares combine well and retain the important right angles. Circular shapes may be used for emphasis.
- Select plants for their form and texture and set them in large expanses or blocks with low ground cover providing a carpet of foliage into which hedges and specimen plants can be placed. Flowers can add specific colour highlights.
- Retain a sense of open space in the garden, with screens and hedges used as freestanding elements. Gaps between these features or sometimes within them provide glimpses of spaces beyond. The idea is to suggest enclosure rather than to create it fully.
- Ensure that the garden layout remains informal and asymmetric with large areas of paving alongside smaller. The organization of the layout should feel random, and patterns should not be repeated.
- Allow paved areas to overlap especially if you have steps or level changes. This enhances the links and movement within the garden.
- Position sculpture or containers asymmetrically, so they catch the eye but do not form a central focal point.
- Choose low, elegant loungers and occasional tables. Dining furniture should be simple and geometric in design.

Key garden designers using a Modernist style: Christopher Bradley-Hole, Tom Stuart-Smith, Andrew Wilson

can be rendered for a smooth surface.

The aim is to minimize or hide fixings and to maximize surface areas. By making each step overhang the next one, such heavy materials appear almost to 'float'.

Colour in Modernist gardens

Surface colours should be neutral or in strong hues. Some renders can be coloured with natural pigments, but most will be painted to produce the finish. Water is used as a reflective surface or is sometimes seen with vertical jets or bubble fountains.

▶ **Sharply defined, often rectilinear** geometry has been combined with asymmetry and informal planting. The minimal detailing emphasizes the surface finishes.

... planting is designed for foliage interest and contrasts...

… urban style is geometric and linked closely to the house…

Urban approach

The majority of small gardens are urban in nature, and this style has grown out of their cosmopolitan character. Although some gardeners respond to the hard architecture of towns and cities by creating heavily planted spaces, there are many more who use their gardens just for leisure and pleasure. In these gardens architectural character dominates.

Flexibility is key to urban gardens as a limited space may need to accommodate a children's play area as well as an area to relax and entertain. Although planting is important, it is just one of many materials used to add character and interest.

Precise layout

Urban gardens share a simple and clear geometric layout and often link closely with the house. Bifolding or sliding, glazed doors minimize the threshold between interior and exterior space to provide a single and expanded living space in warmer periods. Materials are selected to match interior finishes. Furniture, sculpture and ornamentation are often linked or co-ordinated as if in an interior room, and their repetition sets up rhythm and order. Lighting is important in creating atmosphere.

Planting is selected from a simplified palette often chosen for architectural form or textures. Pleached hedging or narrow-canopied trees such as *Carpinus betulus* 'Frans Fontaine' are planted for vertical interest and privacy. Simple mixes of groundcover plants are supplemented by key specimens for drama and

◀ **Bold, dynamic planting** and quirky surfaces comprise the extremes of urban style. This flexible extension to the house is for relaxation and inspiration.

focal interest. Ornamental grass is valued for its transparency and light-capturing qualities. Vertical planting is popular as it enables floor space to be maximized without the loss of plants.

Hardscaping

Decking is frequently used for surfaces or alternatively high-quality stone such as basalt, limestone or sandstone with a sawn or honed finish. Walls and boundaries have smooth rendering or horizontal, slatted timber panels to tie in with the interior house walls.

Furniture is selected for high impact and often used sculpturally within the garden. Clever or hidden storage within furniture or beneath decking is common.

7 ways to create an urban garden

- Maximize space and retain an architectural quality to the surfaces and structures within an urban garden. Keep layout simple with a clearly defined geometry.
- Garden lighting should conjure a theatrical mood after dark as well as allow the garden to be enjoyed from indoors.
- Use columnar or narrowly spreading trees, pleached hedges or pergolas to separate off private areas.
- Repeat key elements such as specimen plants, furniture or containers in order to generate a sense of rhythm and coherence within the garden.
- Rendered walls can be painted for dramatic colour effects. Bear in mind that enlivening, warmer colours from the red-orange spectrum will visually reduce the space. Colours from the cool, blue spectrum will increase the sense of space by suggesting depth.
- Minimize the planting palette by concentrating on simple ground cover into which more dramatic specimens or colour planting can be introduced.
- Water can be combined with sculpture or used to create reflective surfaces (see pp154–155). The installation of underground reservoirs for above-ground water features will occupy less space.

Key garden designers using an urban style: Andy Sturgeon, Philip Nixon, James Aldridge

A row of wind turbines above a yew hedge adds a level of industrial screening to this urban garden and conceals the work area where recycling and composting occur.

... the garden takes on the nature of a theatrical set...

Rescued timber has been used for the boundary and backdrop to this garden to evoke previous uses and incarnations. The *Prunus serrula* bark echoes the mahogany tones.

Conceptualist approach

Concepts are ideas used by creative designers or artists to inform and guide their work, as a focus for their thinking. At their core, concept gardens are therefore expressive, spatial compositions.

Conceptual design in gardens became important toward the end of the 20th century, shifting the focus away from horticulture to one with a direct link to art. The result is exciting and engaging, producing gardens with personality and energy. Recent design shows at Chaumont-sur-Loire in France and the Jardins de Métis/ Reford Gardens in Canada have championed this garden approach.

Where do the ideas originate?

Concepts are derived from historical events or locations, individual or personal characteristics, art itself in its many forms or whimsical thoughts and ideas. Materials are frequently chosen to emphasize particular colours, textures or characteristics – concrete, steel, rubber, Perspex and painted surfaces. Lighting is used for atmospheric compositions.

Conceptualist gardens can be functional spaces, but are often designed to be viewed from a terrace or from an interior vantage point.

How does planting fit in?

Planting can be spectacular if used to express the central idea of the garden rather than to form particular habitats or associations (see p185). Gardens can be planted with a single species or often the strong flower colour of annuals reinforces a colour theme.

▶ **Reflective water** and transparent Perspex play visual tricks with this dining table, which doubles as an aquarium, shimmering with light and the jewelled glow of goldfish.

6 ways to create a conceptualist garden

- At the early planning stage, identify the key word or phrase that sums up the basic concept for the new design. Diffuse, intense, taut or protect are good examples of feelings that might kick-start your thought processes.
- Once the concept is defined use its key words to help you settle on the layout, materials and planting palettes.
- Simplify ideas and options as much as possible to allow the garden to resonate and communicate. It doesn't matter if others don't understand the concepts you have used – the space should entice or fascinate.
- Man-made materials are often found in a conceptualist garden, to allow colour to be a strong, communicative tool. Surfaces of resin-bonded materials or chipped rubber may emphasize this characteristic and intensify the experience.
- Planting may be absent or used to reinforce concepts. Sometimes this may be complex, but often simple expanses of one or two carefully chosen species may be used. Often strident or bold colour, texture and three-dimensional form are key characteristics here.
- View the garden more as an installation than a horticultural endeavour. Express your personality and preferences rather than trying to conform.

Key garden designers using a conceptualist style: Topher Delaney, Vladimir Sitta, Tony Smith

◀ **A combination of formal,** compartmentalized layouts and deep, richly planted, mixed or herbaceous borders typifies the Arts and Crafts style.

The Arts and Crafts approach

The Arts and Crafts movement grew out of a desire to retain artisan skills thought to be under threat from industrial mass production. It was most popular in Britain, where the industrial revolution had been born.

This was a wide-ranging movement in architecture and design, but in its gardens a style was set that influenced garden design for most of the 20th century. For many it remains the epitome of the English garden.

The famous partnership of Gertrude Jekyll and Sir Edwin Lutyens produced some of the most famous and beguiling examples of this style. Cottage-garden planting, local materials and vernacular architecture lie at its heart, although Jekyll introduced classical Italian elements to Lutyens and a Mediterranean palette of planting to their gardens.

Establishing enclosures

Typically Arts and Crafts gardens are enclosed spaces or a series of enclosures formed by walls or more commonly hedges. Each of these outdoor compartments would have a different character.

Planting was rich and luxuriant and often colour-themed either as long herbaceous borders of changing colour sequences or as individual colour-themed gardens such as the White Garden at Sissinghurst, in Kent, or the Hot Garden at Hidcote Manor, in Gloucestershire, both in the UK.

The high point of these original planting schemes was summer, and gardens were generally large enough to sustain a wide range of seasonal planting combinations. Designers such as Rosemary Verey and Penelope Hobhouse championed this approach, which became known as the English flower garden style.

As labour costs increased, the planting in Arts and Crafts gardens changed from mainly herbaceous to mixed borders of perennials and shrubs.

The hardscaping

Paving was of natural stone, normally Yorkstone or local sandstones, which develop an uneven or riven surface as they weather. Local brick, tiles or stone would be used for walls, and timber for structures such as arbours or summerhouses. The patina and character essential to create an Arts and Crafts atmosphere was supplied by second-hand materials.

Adapting to a small garden

This style is ideal for long, narrow gardens where a sequence of enclosures can readily be set up, for different seasonal interest or uses. Mark out these areas with hedges and plant perennials densely to achieve soft, rich contrasts.

▲ **Decorative terra-cotta pots** were favoured by Arts and Crafts designers such as Gertrude Jekyll. The skill involved in their decoration fits perfectly with this particular style.

▼ **Natural materials** and hand-crafted, locally sourced detailing were popular with the Arts and Crafts movement, which influenced many gardens in the 20th century.

7 ways to create an Arts and Crafts garden

- Make the layout formal and often symmetrical, with rectangles dominant. Use circular shapes where paths intersect or change direction.
- Separate different areas of the garden with hedges or low walls.
- Colour theme the planting and emphasize it mainly through flower colour. Foliage coloration can also be used in this way. Single-colour-themed gardens remain popular. White flowers and green foliage work well, especially in shade. A single hue however can reduce visual interest.
- Use natural materials as much as possible. Gravel is an ideal material for low-cost paths, and these can be edged in stone or brick. Cobblestone mosaics are also popular.
- Allow lichens and mosses to invade joints and crevices, creating a patina and a sense of age.
- Choose timber furniture, and let it become silvery with age.
- Adapt ideas and design devices from some of the original Arts and Crafts gardens. Even though the gardens were large in scale, their use of small spaces within the gardens translates well to a small garden.

Key garden designers using an Arts and Crafts style: Penelope Hobhouse, Mary Keen, Fiona Lawrenson

... planting is a
vibrant mix of
perennials and
shrubs...

The cottage-garden style has become universally admired as an approach that combines colourful plantsmanship with an easy informality and charm.

Cottage-garden approach

Originally a cottage garden would have been a series of rectangular beds solely for growing food, to supplement meagre wages. Here and there, hedgerow escapes such as primroses, larkspur and honeysuckle would grow among the crops.

As times became more affluent this concept changed and was romanticized by urban dwellers into a plant-rich heaven in which a huge variety of species would be grown in random profusion with little sense of definition or structure. It is this informality that appeals to gardeners as a celebration of planting itself.

Style characteristics

Planting is a vibrant mix of perennials and shrubs (see also p175). Especially valued for their informality are scented species of roses, mock orange (*Philadelphus*) or lilac (*Syringa*).

Paths are often narrow and the planting is so dominant that the garden layout is subsumed beneath layers of foliage and flowers. To counteract this, clipped hedges and topiaried forms introduce contrast and differentiate areas or add privacy. Narrow views or openings are cut into hedges to create a sense of intrigue.

Chimney pots and barrels are used alongside terra-cotta pots for planting. Furniture is often aged timber or decorative metal, or both materials.

Focus on decoration

Although fruit and vegetables remain a feature, it is now common to see crops mixed with ornamental species. Sweet peas (*Lathyrus*), dahlias and chrysanthemums are grown for cutting, while broad or runner beans are trained on tall frames to dominate the mass of planting.

6 ways to create a cottage garden

- Keep your garden layout simple so the plants really shine. Beds and layouts that are overcomplex will lose legibility.
- Arrange a wide variety of plants in dense, small groups or drifts, for an informal, random look. Consider scent in your plant selection too. Maintenance costs are likely to be high with so many plants.
- Encourage plants to self-seed into crevices and between paving, thereby spreading their unruly charm.
- Use fine-textured species such as box (*Buxus*) and yew (*Taxus baccata*) for hedges and topiary. They will contrast well with the profusion of foliage and flowers that is characteristic of a cottage garden.
- Paving is generally natural materials such as second-hand or weathered stone, granite setts and gravel, laid in random patterns. Brick and tiles may also be introduced when an informal mixture of materials is required.
- Add height within beds and borders with tall plants such as delphiniums, foxgloves (*Digitalis*) or verbascums. Train roses and clematis up vertical plant supports within the borders or up the walls or fences.

Key garden designers using a cottage-garden style: Jinny Blom, Bunny Guinness, Roger Platts

The planting here is modelled on Hidcote Manor, in Gloucestershire, UK, and celebrates the cottage-garden style pioneered by Lawrence Johnston in the early 20th century.

Japanese approach

Japanese gardens assume a wide range of characteristics and design philosophies. However the rich contemporary scene in Japanese garden design breaks with the traditional ethos while retaining a distinct Japanese personality.

The characteristic that the majority of Japanese gardens share is their exploitation of limited space. The functional aspects of the Western garden as a space to use are countered by a more spiritual purpose in which asymmetrical composition is paramount. These gardens often take on the quality of spatial sculpture.

Balancing density

Asymmetry is key. Objects, plants or surfaces are balanced by relative density or transparency, weight, texture or colour. In general, foliage and surface textures are emphasized and combined for contrast (see also p179). Characterful boulders, gravel or combined paving textures are set against soft mosses or still, reflective water. Vertical plants such as irises

▲ **Keep ornamentation** such as lanterns or water basins to a minimum. As key focal points they work well when set against simple foliage textures.

▲ **Water is used** as a cleansing and symbolic element in Japanese gardens. Here narrow paths cross reflective pools in this courtyard garden, contributing to a thought-provoking and reflective experience.

and grasses balance massed, low ground cover or heavily pruned pines.

Often contorted or gnarled specimen plants are favoured, creating a sense of abstracted wildness – the essence of nature captured in a restricted space. In Zen gardens this is taken to an extreme, minimalist landscape of raked gravel and composed rock arrangements.

Contemporary Japanese gardens are also often more sculptural, using expanses of hard materials or water with carefully chosen specimen plants.

Boundaries

These are important in Japanese gardens not least because they are so evident in smaller spaces. Bamboo screens are often used for decorative boundaries, while planting may hide or disguise the peripheries and link into the surrounding planting beyond

the garden. In this way the garden becomes a small oasis or clearing within a wider landscape.

Creating movement

If used, paths are indirect and the textured surfaces intentionally difficult to negotiate. This creates a purposeful sense of movement, and focal points or incidents are introduced at key junctions or changes of direction. Such routes would have been used in association with the ancient tea ceremonies, which included water as a means of purification and preparation. Stone basins for catching or holding fresh water were set in key locations.

▲ **An eye for finer details** will add the finishing touches to a Japanese garden. Attention to asymmetric but balanced arrangements is typical of this style.

6 ways to create a Japanese garden

- Make the layout asymmetric and design the garden so it is either best viewed from the house or main terrace or when walked through, taking into account specific views or key plants or artifacts.
- Select specimen plants such as maples (*Acer*) or pines (*Pinus*), which are often multistemmed or naturally assume gnarled and contorted forms. They will contribute to the age and character of the garden, while many other plants are painstakingly pruned to look old and knobbly.
- Trim mass-planted, groundcover shrubs into soft, organic forms.
- Introduce water as an incidental feature in stone basins or as a more extensive reflective surface.
- Gravel is the key textured surface against which plants and boulders are displayed. In Zen gardens a particularly fine grade of gravel is raked into clear, organic patterns.
- Use ornament sparingly if at all, and keep the whole composition simple, with open space balancing solid and planted elements (see p46).

Key garden designers using a Japanese style: Haruko Seki, Shodo Suzuki, Takeshi Nagasaki

... the essence of nature in a restricted space...

The use of contrast is important in much Japanese garden design. Here the precarious balance of the tortured pine is silhouetted against luminous, white walls.

... relaxed but heavy with fragrance and strong colour...

Mediterranean approach

There has long been something of a love affair between the Mediterranean region and garden designers, particularly for the wilder regions where maquis vegetation dominates. These gravelly, windswept landscapes are now home to many of the staple plants – from euphorbia to lavender and rosemary – to be found in gardens and herb collections elsewhere in the world.

Informality is key

A charming, relaxed atmosphere percolates these gardens, which are heavy with their fragrance and strong colouring. Planting is informally or even randomly arranged in groups or associations, mirroring the sun-bleached original habitat (see p177).

Trees such as olives, fig or bay laurel are planted for their height and to give light shade, while lavender, rosemary, yucca, euphorbia and thyme cover the ground. Many Mediterranean species bear grey or glaucous foliage, which intensifies the character of these dry landscapes.

Growing through gravel

Most areas in a Mediterranean garden are covered with gravel, including the main planting beds. Plants emerge or self-seed in this textured surface. Smaller areas of paving for terraces or seating areas can be designed using slabs of stone or terra cotta. Rustic paving slabs are also suitable for open-jointed crazy paving.

Boundaries can be rendered and sometimes decorated with tiles. Keep colour washes either in neutral or

◀ **Lines of lavender,** sitting in limestone gravel, are evocative of sun-warmed days and herb-perfumed air, while olive trees shade the invading perennials below.

▲ **Heavily perfumed climbers** such as *Trachelospermum jasminoides* thrive when planted against a sunny wall. Colourful tiles and warm terra-cotta colours evoke a Mediterranean character.

6 ways to create a Mediterranean garden

- Use gravel across the entire garden if possible with the exception of any paved terraces. Even here joints can be filled with gravel. Lay some geotextile below the gravel to prevent weed infestation from the soil below.
- Limestone is the most appropriate hard paving material because it is the native stone of much of the Mediterranean region.
- Select specimen trees and shrubs that look weather-beaten or interestingly knobbly. Multistemmed specimens work particularly well in creating a sense of architecture within the garden.
- Randomize the planting so that there is no specific rhythm or pattern to the garden. Some plants can be densely grouped, while others can be single specimens as if the plants had self-seeded.
- Allow weeds and seeds to take root in the gravel. Although gravel is generally low in maintenance, you will have to watch for and weed out more aggressive species.
- Check on the hardiness of some species such as olive or cypress as they may be prone to frost or snow damage. Plants propagated and grown on in your home country will often prove hardier than imported species.

Key garden designers using a Mediterranean style: John Brookes, Anthony Paul, Debbie Roberts and Ian Smith of Acres Wild

earth tones or add occasional blocks of stronger colour.

Mosaics of coloured tiles or cobbles are typical of Mediterranean gardens, and plants self-seed within this paving, colonizing whole areas.

Mediterranean character

Planting areas are designed so that they can be walked through and concealed seating areas discovered, to form casual retreats.

Water may be introduced in small bubble fountains or brimming containers. Alternatively, think of using narrow rills to carry water through the garden. Boulders or terra-cotta pots also form focal points.

DIY DESIGN

Applying colour

- Certain colours are perceived as being hot (reds and oranges) while others are cooler (blues and greens).
- Grade flower hues from intense to pale along the length of a flowerbed or border, to exaggerate distance.
- Intense colour in small spaces can be dramatic but visually tiring. Red for example will make a space seem smaller. Use bold colour sparingly against a more neutral backdrop.
- The fiery and warmer colours of orange, red-orange and red can be chosen to add emphasis to foreground colour, while blues, greens and blue-purples can be used for background depth. Foliage can also be manipulated in this way.

... materials can be rescued, recycled or found locally...

Ecological approach

This approach is more of a philosophy than a style, and it concentrates on making gardens work as communities or habitats rather than as merely decorative spaces. The related issues of sustainability and climate change have now brought this garden philosophy into sharp focus.

The study of how and where plants grow and how they co-exist produces a different emphasis when the goal is planting a garden. Plant choice in these circumstances is often confused with the sole use of native species, but ecology in its wider sense enables plants from similar habitats and

conditions to be combined, potentially mixing native and imported species.

Minimal intervention

This is achieved in the garden by balancing competition between selected species, and by matching

◀ **Sustainable prairie planting** here includes a succession of echinaceas, rudbeckias, asters and *Panicum virgatum*. Such dense but colourful planting needs little maintenance.

species to the prevailing conditions rather than attempting to alter them, through the addition of fertilizers for example. Aggressive, spreading plants or prolific self-seeders are left off the plant list.

Sourcing materials

Select recycled or locally sourced hardscaping, thus reducing transportation and the carbon footprint. Renewable resources such as timber from managed and approved plantations are also appropriate.

Storing water

Water is an increasingly precious resource, and measures for its conservation, storage and absorption are integral to the ecological approach. Collect rainwater off the roof into water butts or underground storage tanks. Swale planting is an alternative in which water absorption is controlled by suitable wetland planting. Green roof planting will absorb and slow the flow of rainwater on rooftops creating a more measured drainage cycle. Filtration planting for the cleaning of grey water should also be considered.

6 ways to create an ecological garden

- Create as many habitats as possible to increase biodiversity within a garden. In a small garden it may be worth joining forces with neighbours so you have a series of habitat-specific gardens, rather than trying to do everything in a limited space.
- Allow space for composting both garden and kitchen waste. Also allocate an area for log storage, which can provide an important habitat for overwintering insects.
- Transform roofs by fitting them with preplanted sedum matting. New-build houses and extensions might be able to accommodate more elaborate green roof systems.
- Treat water as a potential habitat, rather than a purely decorative feature, by introducing marginal and aquatic planting to lure additional wildlife.
- Select paving, garden furniture and other garden items from the increasing range of recycled products, many of which offer sophisticated designs. It is possible to create an elegant and stylish design solution with ecological credentials.
- Sow perennial and annual seed mixes, which have a low carbon footprint and are inexpensive yet give great results. Successional interest to give prolonged seasonal impact is built into many designed mixtures.

Key garden designers using an ecological style: James Hitchmough, Nigel Dunnett, Noel Kingsbury

---

DIY DESIGN

Create 'ecotones' to increase wildlife

- The more habitats you can provide, the more diverse the wildlife interest will be in your garden.
- Some species will settle into the specific habitats you recreate: for example, a bog garden or meadow,
- A wide range of animals and invertebrates thrive in the junctions between these habitats. These are known as ecotones.
- Establish a woodland-edge planting of trees, shrubs and taller grasses, as a whole woodland is impossible to fit into a small garden. This should act as an ecotone and connect to bog planting, marginals and aquatics and so significantly increase biodiversity within a restricted space.

Exotic approach

For some cities in cool-temperate regions it is unusual to experience serious frost and snow. In such man-made microclimates you can grow a range of subtropical plants in an exotic-style garden. Although many are not fully hardy, the warmer and protected conditions of the small urban garden create niche conditions that many urban gardeners celebrate.

Dominant themes

Planting is king in these gardens. Bold foliage is typical of the dense, junglelike planting, and is provided by large-leaved bananas, loquats (*Eriobotrya japonica*) or *Fatsia japonica*.

Strong colour is found in cannas or dahlias, while taller grasses can lend movement and transparency to the

▶ **A lively mixture** of yellow-stemmed *Phyllostachys aureosulcata* f. *aureocaulis*, phormiums and palms provide some much-needed privacy in this small garden.

... create junglelike effects with bold foliage...

DIY DESIGN

Jungle plants for drama

- Select large-leaved and more exotic plants for their eye-catching qualities in your garden.
- Make bold foliage gestures with the large, fleshy leaves of banana (*Musa*).
- Tall canna lilies bring warm splashes of colour bubbling from finely striped or glossy, burgundy foliage. Protect their rhizomes in winter with a thick mulch, or else lift and overwinter them under glass.
- Bamboos introduce height and fine foliage textures, often whispering or gently rustling in the breeze. *Phyllostachys nigra* has black stems and *P. aureosulcata* f. *aureocaulis* produces bright yellow ones.

6 ways to create an exotic garden

- Keep paths narrow to add mystery or trick the eye into thinking they lead to cool, shaded destinations.
- Plant densely in order to lose boundaries and spread ambiguity. The actual size of the garden can be hidden completely.
- Note the hardiness of the plants in which you are interested. Some specimen plants or more unusual species may need winter protection.
- Introduce additional colour with summer annuals, which can be moved around the garden in containers. More tender species can also be more easily protected this way.
- Source idiosyncratic furniture and containers – perhaps exotic single pieces, which can sometimes be found in architectural salvage yards. Alternatively focus on a particular location such as Thailand or Central America and furnish the exotic garden accordingly.
- Lay natural materials to cover the ground. Timber decking is a good option as it is always warm underfoot. Riven or rusticated stone in crazed form is also typical.

Key garden designers using an exotic style: Declan Buckley, Raymond Jungles, Will Giles

scene. Bamboos can flourish beside palms to give height and privacy.

Paving and walls

Grow climbers such as the trumpet vine (*Campsis*) or large-leaved ivy (*Hedera*) on boundary walls. Rendered walls painted with strong colours contrast well with the bold thickets.

Paving can be simple areas or paths of gravel, or else decking and rustic stone. Large ceramic pots add decoration and colour, while splashing water raises humidity levels and adds a mysterious sound.

▶ **The huge split leaves** of banana establish an exotic feel. In cool-temperate climates even the hardiest species, *Musa basjoo*, needs protection from severe cold.

CREATING A STYLE

This original design by Tom Stuart-Smith for a private
London client exemplifies how a house and its main living
spaces can be tied visually to the garden.

The architecture of this modernized
town house transforms the
relationship between the house and
garden. A tall, double-storey window
allows the garden to be enjoyed
from the main living spaces, and the
architectural treatment of the garden
by Tom Stuart-Smith responds to this
sense of continuity.

Wide glass doors open out onto
the terrace with a continuous level
surface that diffuses the threshold
between the interior and exterior. The
dark concrete is a neutral surface that
becomes reflective when wet.

Planting and paths

A restricted palette of tree ferns,
hakonechloas and box form the
planting character of the garden,
with *Hydrangea anomala* subsp.
petiolaris covering the boundary wall.
The playfulness of the meandering
path invites exploration to the higher
levels, where seating, storage and a
children's play area are located.

Hints of Modernism

Echoes of Modernism run through
the garden, as shown by the use of
concrete, and a horizontally slatted
timber fence emphasizing the
horizontal/vertical simplicity of the
main window. Pure drama is derived
from the reduction of complexity in
favour of design clarity.

▶ **Wide and simple glass doors** open onto
a smooth concrete terrace, which matches
the internal floor finish to blur the boundary
between interior and garden.

Design ideas to take home

- Planting has been selected for
  eye-catching texture and form,
  and contrasts well with the
  simple surfaces and materials.
- Dyed concrete and narrow-
  slatted hardwood fencing give
  lateral emphasis.
- Clear connection has been
  made with the architecture
  of the building, so the garden
  and house can be enjoyed as
  a single entity.
- Local brick has been used to
  match the materials of the
  house and to relate to the wider
  context of the garden.
- Playful gravel paths wind
  through the garden to separate
  seating and play spaces.

...a dramatic contrast between Modernist materials and textured planting...

MODERNIST JUNGLE

The fine hardwood timber slatting (1) cladding the high boundary wall forms a uniform backdrop to this urban, cool-temperate garden. Climbers will eventually soften and green this feature.

Tree ferns (*Dicksonia antarctica*) (2) stand like sculptures within the space, providing a tall but transparent canopy that diffuses light and enhances privacy.

A low-textured carpet of the shade-loving grass *Hakonechloa macra* (3) gives a soft, wave-like feel to the planted areas, through which clipped spherical specimens of box (*Buxus sempervirens*) (4) emerge in randomized groups.

The dark-dyed, smooth concrete used on the terrace (5) is reflective after rain showers.

◀ **Narrow gravel paths** meander through the garden, linking the main terrace with a timber deck at the end of the garden, which has been designed as an area for play and relaxation.

SMALL GARDEN

MATERIALS

It is the hard materials that give a garden its main structure, providing a stable surface on which to walk, work and relax. They can also evoke or define a design style, enhance the atmosphere and introduce permanent colour and texture.

Materials should be introduced sparingly to bring much needed unity and coherence to the garden. Typically only three or four materials should be used within a garden to enhance its sense of consistency, against which the planting plays out its drama.

Historically hardscaping was limited to natural materials but an increasingly wide range of natural and man-made materials are now finding their way into our gardens, bringing dramatic colours, textures and finishes.

15 ways to... exploit materials

1. Keep things simple

Limit the range of hard materials that you select, especially in smaller garden spaces. The use of a single material for paving, for example, will make the area appear larger than it in fact is.

2. Consider scale

Small-scale materials such as setts or cobblestones work well in small spaces or 'rooms', because they increase textural detail. Meanwhile larger slabs will simplify the space and add a greater sense of drama.

3. Use the architecture

Think of the house or apartment façade as an integral part of the garden. You can relate its materials to your paving or the garden boundary, perhaps picking up on colour washes too for rendered surfaces.

4. Build foundations

All surfaces and structures built within a garden need some form of foundation for stability and support. They must therefore be considered as an integral part of any garden design even though these elements are no longer visible once the garden has been completed.

5. Get technical

Take care when selecting your hardscaping. Paving materials in particular have to be stronger than building ones as they are permanently damp due to contact with the ground and can be affected by freezing conditions. Use only paving-quality bricks as they are dense enough to resist frost shattering, unlike weaker house bricks.

6. Check levels

The height of the paved surfaces within a garden will have major implications on the buildings they serve. Most properties will have a damp-proof layer of some description included in their construction, and paving must be laid below this damp-proof level to prevent rising damp within the property.

7. Taking care of rainwater drainage

Rainwater needs to drain off paved surfaces. These are therefore laid to 'falls' – subtle gradients that ensure that water runs away effectively. It is essential that water always drains in the correct direction, that is, away from the property into the garden, in order to reduce the risk of water penetrating the house.

8. Install underground water storage

Some paving systems include subsurface water storage. Legislation in some countries dictates that water runoff in front gardens must be managed or contained in some way to reduce the risk of urban flooding.

9. Research services

Most gardens will include services of one form or another. Typically drains taking sewage from the house will cut across the garden and will frequently

13. Erect ramps

Ramps allow access for all users as well as gradual changes in level. They take up considerably more space than steps however and need to be carefully integrated into the design.

14. Install lighting

Lights add an extra dimension to the garden, not only extending its use after dark in the summer months but also revealing the garden when viewed through a house window on other occasions during the year. Keeping the lighting design simple and minimal increases the dramatic effect.

15. Discover new materials

A wide range of materials is now available for garden use, many of which are man-made and colourful. These materials can transform urban gardens and introduce long-lasting colour throughout the year. Try to source such hardscaping locally if at all possible, because this reduces the carbon footprint and supports your local economy. Many artists and craftsmen specialize in such garden commissions.

10. Choose permeable surfaces

In urban gardens especially it is important to consider the use of permeable paving materials and systems. This allows rainwater to pass through into the ground below rather than into the mains drains.

include an inspection chamber where drains change direction. Such inspection chambers enable blockages to be accessed from the surface, but their covers can create awkward interruptions to paving. However they should never be paved over or ignored.

11. Design steps

Assess step design carefully because steps can be hazardous. External steps are lower and wider than internal ones. As single steps can be easily missed, it is better to have more than one step at a time.

12. Match furniture

Aim to co-ordinate your garden furniture to suit the materials palette and style that you wish to achieve. Approach the selection as you would a sculpture – furniture should be decorative and functional.

Materials as a design tool

The seemingly endless array of materials available for use within the garden can make the selection process daunting. By thinking through your options first however, the design process can be simplified considerably.

Fulfilling a function

The hard surfaces in a garden stabilize the ground and provide a long-lasting platform so that the garden can be enjoyed safely in virtually any weather. They also prevent soil erosion to well-used routes such as those to the garden shed and compost heap. The space immediately outside the kitchen door is likely to become especially worn if not protected by paving.

The provision of a solid surface is also invaluable for garden furniture, containers and sculptures, as it spreads the load across a wider area and makes the movement of chairs and tables easier. Textured surfaces prevent or reduce slip, while drainage falls shed excess water from the surface to reduce standing water and speed up the drying process.

▲ **Timber is a versatile** material. Hardwoods can be left to silver with age or be stained and painted to introduce colour and drama.

Steps and boundaries

Steps and ramps made in hard materials can be used for slopes and level changes. Such materials are also excellent to build screens and vertical structures. Boundaries contribute to a clear sense of ownership and provide privacy. Within the garden freestanding walls and screens can be sited so that they block unsightly views or disguise storage facilities.

Permanent character

Quite apart from their usefulness, hardscaping materials have their own aesthetic qualities and bring a special sense of permanent character to a garden. Such materials may be chosen for their colour. For example light paving materials such as limestone reflect light into the garden and can brighten even the shadiest corner. When placed alongside the house this material will also direct light into the interior. Darker paving materials such as basalt or granite not only quieten the atmosphere and mood but also emphasize planting colour. In wet conditions such dark surfaces become more reflective too. Painted render, powder-coated metals and reflective surfaces can establish much livelier colour combinations.

For smooth and simple surfaces include only a minimal number of textures. Stone can be sawn or honed to create a regular surface that suits

◄ **Paved surfaces are essential** for paths in areas of heaviest use.

▶ **A coherent colour palette** permeates this courtyard garden, creating a subtle sense of drama. The combination of lawn and stone paving strips softens the effect.

architectural and geometric layouts. Riven paving or flame-textured surfaces have a much richer patina and a more diverse visual interest. The play of light and shade across these surfaces can be fascinating. Other smaller paving materials such as cobbles, setts and gravel introduce textures either through their nature as gravels or aggregates or by the way in which they are laid as small units. Jointing patterns in themselves can be highly decorative.

Design counterpoint

Materials can be chosen to blend with or match those of the house or the surrounding area, while a noticeably different material will emphasize the counterpoint and add a sense of excitement.

DIY DESIGN

The rules of repetition

A key design tool to simplify and co-ordinate a garden's planting scheme is to use repetition.

- Select key plants with a common design character, perhaps height, foliage colour or branching pattern. Plant each key species in several places but beside each one introduce a different species every time, for variety.
- Use simple, clipped forms of box (*Buxus*) in containers at strategic locations so that all pot-grown plants are the same and the main borders provide the variety.
- Keep the number of paving materials to a minimum and repeat details or paving patterns at key points in the garden. Closely match the paving colour for any painted surfaces.

How to choose your materials

As paving forms an essential part of your garden layout and is a long-term investment, you should give careful thought to your choice.

Pick your paving

Paving slabs, sometimes called flag stones, are available in two forms – natural stone or man-made – and are almost always rectangular or square. Such shapes are easily laid in regular patterns with little wastage. It is possible to find slabs in different shapes, and some specialist companies will cut these to order.

Natural stone paving

Stone slabs are typically sandstone, limestone, granite or basalt but a wider range of options is available from across the world. More recently so-called 'New World' stone has become available from India, China and South America. The sourcing and performance of these new materials need to be carefully considered. All stone should be bought through reputable suppliers who can clarify ethical issues such as the use of child labour, the carbon footprint of imported materials and the hardiness of these materials in your climate. Some materials will absorb moisture and shatter in freezing conditions.

Yorkstone

Traditionally Yorkstone has been used in gardens in the UK. This is a sandstone derived from the Peak District, and it varies in colour from honey or buff through to grey and blue. As it ages, Yorkstone delaminates to form a riven surface, as do other locally sourced sandstones as well as much of the stone imported from India. Like all stones Yorkstone can be sawn or honed to have a smooth finish for contemporary schemes.

Some other natural stones can be flame textured to produce an artificially delaminated surface or a textured surface that is safer. Natural stone is generally an expensive choice of material although many imported materials are competitively priced.

◄ **Stone or concrete slabs** are available in a range of sizes, colours and finishes. Here they are laid in a random pattern.

Man-made paving

Because Yorkstone is expensive both in new and second-hand form, many concrete manufacturers seek to emulate the riven appearance of this stone as it weathers in order to offer more competitively priced materials that share at least some of Yorkstone's characteristics. The dyes used to

▲ **Old Yorkstone is used** here to create an informal sitting area. The random pattern of weathered and textured stones establishes a softer, rustic quality.

make such concrete paving are rarely colourfast in sunlight and the repetition of surface patterns can draw attention to the fact that the stone has been artificially processed. This may not however be a drawback.

In situ concrete

Concrete is an ancient man-made material although it is often associated with more modern times. The key ingredients are sand, cement and aggregate (or gravel), which when mixed with water produce a sludge-like liquid that sets to become concrete. The liquid concrete can be poured into a mould either laid on the ground to form paving or held vertically to create walls. For structures and larger expanses of paving, steel reinforcement gives extra strength. Because it is poured in place this concrete is called *in situ* concrete.

The versatility of concrete

The liquid nature of the concrete before it sets means that it will fill any mould or formwork, and as a result curved and irregularly angled shapes can be manufactured as well as squares and rectangles. Thus concrete is a versatile material with a wide range of uses, and its surface can be textured and finished in the same way as precast material.

Large slabs of concrete are made up to 6 x 6m (20 x 20ft), but concrete

▲ **Poured concrete can be** formed into virtually any shape for paving that is complemented by a wide range of surface finishes.

will expand when hot and contract when cool so that expansion joints between larger slabs are needed to prevent cracking. The joints can be gravel or narrow planting strips. Whether or not you can introduce *in situ* concrete may be determined by your garden's accessibility to the machinery used to make and pour it.

Concrete paving

Concrete in slab form, or what is known as precast, can also take on a wide range of finishes from smooth and semipolished to textured or patterned. In a product known as 'exposed aggregate concrete' the fine particles are washed away before the concrete dries to reveal the aggregate as a surface finish. This can be highly decorative, and as a naturally pigmented material it will not fade. Because the manufacturing process can be carefully controlled, a high-quality, consistent finish is achieved – unlike natural materials.

▲ **Brick is a traditional** garden material and available in a wide range of colours and textures to suit various garden styles.

▲ **Granite setts can be** used to form intricate and detailed patterns because of their smaller sizes.

Paving brick

Brick has been used for centuries as a paving material as well as for buildings and walls. Old paving blocks, which are known as paviors, would have been laid with mortar joints, for a rigid surface.

More recently, and to compete more successfully with concrete block paving, manufacturers have produced a range of bricks that can be laid into sand with the joints tightly butted together. Sand is brushed into the joints and the whole construction is vibrated and compacted to form the surface. This technique means that the paved surface remains flexible rather than rigid so it needs a retaining edge. Otherwise, with use and over time, the paving blocks could move and the whole surface would disintegrate.

Granite setts

Setts are traditionally small cubes of granite used to pave streets and public squares across Europe. Occasionally granite setts can be found in rectangular blocks. Their small scale means that they are suitable for simple mosaic patterns.

In gardens, setts are often used for paths and as decorative edges to paving or lawns. They make good edgings for loose gravel too.

Man-made block paving

Concrete manufacturers have produced a wide range of brick and sett types for paving use, as a cost-effective alternative to natural stone or brick. Such man-made material is usually bedded into sand and vibrated and compacted to form the paved surface. Interlocking patterns offer the strongest and longest-lasting surfaces.

Go for gravel

Gravel refers to any crushed stone, and it is the most economic paving material for a small garden, especially in its loose form. It is available in different sizes or grades from fine, rounded pea shingle to coarser, angular chippings.

Apart from being an invaluable paving material gravel also makes a good surface mulch to cover planted areas. The mulch, which should be laid over a geotextile or weed-suppressing membrane, helps to retain moisture

in the soil below and can reduce weed growth. No other hard material can be used in this way, combining hard and soft elements. Some of the qualities of a Mediterranean garden can be imitated with gravel mulches, and finer gravels can be raked into patterns in Japanese-style gardens.

Maintaining loose gravel

As a mobile material gravel needs a retaining edge to help keep it in place. Slab or block paving is suitable as an edging material or for greater subtlety use timber or steel edging. Over time, loose gravel will need to be raked and eventually refreshed or topped up.

Bound gravel

For a more stable surface mix gravel with clay and water so it compacts to form bound gravel. This decorative surface is often used as a finishing layer over a coarser material known as hoggin – a mixture of small pebbles, finer particles and clay. These surfaces still require retaining edges as they are flexible rather than rigid.

More recently resin-bound or resin-bonded gravel has become popular. This material is similar in many ways to asphalt but the gravel of your choice is fixed within a clear resin binding agent. This allows its colour to be revealed. Resin-bound gravel is a poured and flexible material so needs a retaining edge to prevent the surface spreading and gradually breaking up. Coloured glass chippings or chipped rubber in brilliant colours can also be laid in this way to create strident colour in the garden.

This spiral wall is faced with textured stone. The wide, flat copings provide additional space for informal seating as well as protecting and finishing the wall.

Add a mowing path to maximize space

A paved surround to the lawn can solve a number of potential problems in a small garden.

- The paving can be a narrow trim or more of a path or route, depending on the space available.
- Maintenance of the lawn edge is reduced as the mower will do the job as you cut the lawn.
- A paved edge stops areas of dead grass where plants from the surrounding borders have flopped over onto the lawn.
- By framing with the same paving materials as the terrace and paths, visually the lawn becomes an integral part of the whole garden rather than a separate element.

Cobbles

The term 'cobbles' refers to pebbles and loose stones that are used as a decorative mulch over planted areas or as 'beaches' in association with ponds or water features.

They also make an excellent paving surface if laid into mortar and look good in mosaic patterns. Their relatively small scale allows them to be introduced in quite intricate schemes. Although to the untrained eye these pebbles seem somewhat formless, they do in fact have direction and character. When set on edge their textured and directional patterns have a combed appearance. When placed on end their narrow points provide dots of colour, and when used flat the cobbles create more organic patterns.

A well-laid cobble mosaic maximizes the material and minimizes the visible mortar holding it in place.

Timber decking

Decking is normally associated with timber, although materials such as steel grilles or narrow slats of paving can be supported on a subframe. Supported decking in roof gardens enables surface water to drain away.

Timber decking is available in two main forms: hardwood and softwood. Softwood is treated to extend its natural life and is generally cheaper than longer-lasting hardwoods, some of which are very hard and resilient.

Decking can be erected across ground that is less prepared or

▲ **Moss-covered stones,** tiles and trickling water contribute to an artful, rustic informality and charm in this shady garden, which is planted mainly for foliage interest.

finished than it would otherwise have to be for a solid, paved surface, thus time and sometimes money are saved. In addition, the decking surface can be aligned with an interior floor level, so there is a continuous surface across the threshold. In the space below the deck air can circulate and dry out any moisture. Although heavy rain will cause some splash against the building this will not cause rising damp in the property walls.

In moist and moderate winters in cool-temperate areas, dampness on shaded timber decking can remain when the temperature is high enough for algae to grow. Such a combination creates slippery conditions.

Height and balustrades

Because a deck is a raised surface it may impinge on your privacy, and you may also require a balustrade for safety reasons.

As rainwater and light can penetrate the deck it is a good idea to add a weed barrier below it to prevent later infestation. Protective grilles or skirtings can also help to deter pests such as rats or foxes from using the deck structure as their home.

▼ **Gabion cages can be** filled with an extensive range of materials such as pebbles to form retaining walls or seats.

▼ **Hardwood decking can be** left untreated to silver with age. Keep shapes and patterns simple to avoid expense in construction.

Hardwood decking combined with
neutral, grey-rendered retaining walls
and evergreen planting introduce a
formal symmetry to this dramatic small
garden with its clean lines.

A raised terrace, with generous sofa, is a focal point in this attractive garden, as well as a platform from which to appreciate the setting. The elegant, sheltering structure combines rich textures with those of the planting.

Tackling changes of level

While no garden is ever completely flat most small gardens will have only minimal slopes. In some situations level changes are voluntarily introduced to establish a focus within the garden or to designate a dining or relaxation area as different and separate. For gardens on slopes, changes in level are invaluable to obtain flat, usable surfaces. These need to have retaining walls and be connected by steps or ramps.

Building steps

Steps are both a delight and a danger. They provide the means of negotiating a level change but for the less able-bodied they represent a barrier to free movement. Steps should be clearly visible and of simple construction. Where possible build at least two steps rather than a single one, which can be easily missed.

As a rule each step should be no higher than 150mm (6in). This is known as the riser height. They should be no less than 300mm (12in) deep – this is known as the tread. In general the greater the tread dimension the lower the riser dimension can be.

Constructing ramps

Ramps provide an alternative way of negotiating level changes and a more gradual means of rising or falling that is accessible for all. For short lengths and minimal level changes build ramps to a gradient of 1:10,

▶ **Although different levels** within a garden create visual interest the need for steps and retaining walls will increase the cost and complexity of construction.

so that it rises 1m (3ft) in height over a 10m (30ft) distance. Because a ramp therefore takes up a considerable amount of space it must be carefully designed in any garden with major level changes, and in some smaller spaces it may be best to remove any level changes altogether.

Making retaining walls

Retaining walls hold back any raised areas of ground that would otherwise collapse. Those below 1m (3ft) in height can be safely built by amateur gardeners as long as good construction methods are followed. For walls more than 1m (3ft) in height it is best to consult a structural engineer. Expert advice is especially important if the garden has clay soil, which can expand and contract as moisture levels vary, and where gardens are surrounded by neighbouring buildings, which could be affected by excavation. In some cases excavations and level changes may be forbidden in close proximity to buildings, and party wall agreements may be required should you wish to carry out this work.

▶ **Retaining walls are necessary** to support major changes in ground level but they can be designed with sufficient depth for seating and decorative display.

The impact of construction in a small garden

The more construction you introduce into your garden the more you need to plan for disruption. Topsoil should be stripped and stored for later re-laying, trenches and formation levels excavated and drainage runs accommodated because paving, walls and fences all need supporting foundations.

In most small gardens this level of disruption can be a practical challenge, and in addition many small gardens are accessed only through the house so all materials must travel through it. For outgoing materials dirt is the biggest concern; for incoming materials it is the size of objects and plants where house doorways restrict heights and widths.

For roof gardens these issues are exacerbated by height and access restrictions, so assess these difficulties before materials are bought. If you are using a contractor, allocate a larger than normal budget to the labour as much of the work will be manual with materials carried in smaller bags.

Decorating the garden

In addition to the basic construction of a garden it is possible to exploit and manipulate other materials in order to increase drama and visual interest, especially now that architecture plays a leading role in influencing the design of our gardens. This relationship means that progressive designs are becoming increasingly colourful and expressive. Therefore stainless steel, corten steel, acrylics, glass and various claddings have found their way into the modern garden.

Materials come of age

A wide variety of stains and paints add to this changing scene, and garden furniture is now available in many styles and materials, as the quality and range of our interior spaces is spilling out of doors.

Sculpture and furniture are now often interchangeable or indistinguishable. Sophisticated outdoor kitchens and stylish barbecues enhance the sense of an inclusive domestic living space rather than a separate interior and exterior. Shared living, cooking and dining spaces in our interiors are also being included in the garden.

Lighting effects

It is important not to overdo lighting in small spaces, yet the ability to paint with highlights and strong shadows can provide some exciting effects. Carefully targeted lighting can energize specimen planting to give dramatic shadows and silhouettes. Subtle uplighting, floor washes or spot lighting are all possible. Light fittings are generally becoming smaller and

▲ **Garden lighting comes** in all shapes and sizes. Choose floor-mounted feature lights for a bold, oriental or industrial character.

more flexible with LED lighting and fibre optics, with their tiny spots of light, creating spectacular effects within paving, walls, decks and steps.

DIY DESIGN

Five tips when lighting a small garden

- The effect of lighting should be seen but not the light fittings themselves.
- Wash vertical surfaces with uplighters for a soft ambient glow that may be sufficient for small spaces.
- Pick out textured surfaces such as brick or stone walls with up- or downlighters to enhance their features.
- Use understep lights if you have level changes. Rope lights can be recessed into grooves under the paved overhangs.
- Spotlight key plants or focal points. Side lighting is effective in revealing form and surface texture, while spots placed in tree canopies create pools of light and branching shadows.

Metals, glass and architectural
materials such as these set a
challenging and dynamic modern tone,
especially in small gardens.

Timber raised beds, decorated with woven willow, are sympathetic materials for this productive kitchen garden. The space between the beds allows for easy access and convenient cropping.

MATERIALS:
CASE STUDY

MASTERING MATERIALS

In his design for this suburban garden, designer John Brookes resolves many of the level issues and difficulties that affect small spaces.

The site is awkwardly shaped with angled boundaries and level changes. Existing orchard trees have been kept to lend a sense of maturity; therefore the original levels were retained.

A new sense of focus to the garden has been supplied by the paved surfaces with their strong rectangular shapes, while the broad planting beds screen the garden boundaries. The centrepiece in the garden is the steps, which invite you to explore the higher levels.

Coherent feel

By maintaining the brick treatment through paving, steps and the pool surround a sense of unity is achieved. The box (*Buxus*) hedging echoes the basic geometry of the site before perennials and larger shrubs soften the design further. Timber seats and terra-cotta planters continue the soft, neutral material tones and provide a backdrop to plant colours and textures.

▲ **A simple brick overhang** creates a shadow line on the steps. Such a 'floating' design emphasizes the level change.

▼ **The composition of light** and shade in this garden is framed by a painted trellis porch enhancing the view into the farthest corners.

Design ideas to take home

- Simplified palette of brick and gravel enables the planting scheme to shine.
- Coherent colour palette of materials – London stock brick and brown beach gravel – gives a uniform feel.
- Good use of level changes without a change in material.
- Overhang on step introduces a shadow line for safety and visual interest, so the bricks can 'float'.
- Strong geometry used throughout the garden to retain a coherent design.
- Small textured items such as bricks provide visual interest without the need for a lawn.

... a hidden delight that gradually reveals its character...

1

2

3

2

4

UNITY AND SIMPLICITY

Clearly defined rectangular paved areas (1) and planting beds (2) here establish a visual focus within an irregular plot. Deep borders and mature trees allow plants to dominate and soften the space.

The paths (3) are wide and generous, and the use of brick in the upper levels allows the seating space to be conveniently patterned, as well as opened up so that the material appears to flow through the entire garden.

The gravel (4), into which plants can self-seed, introduces an informal mood. The colours remain homogeneous, unifying the entire design.

SMALL GARDEN

BOUNDARIES

Boundaries identify ownership and define the garden's extent. In small gardens they can be a limiting feature, obvious and potentially oppressive, because they cast shade. They do however offer privacy – as do screens – although their maximum height may be restricted by your local authority. These opposing considerations should be weighed carefully to find the best solution for your particular plot.

To reduce their impact boundary markers can either be embraced and emphasized or be disguised. A key tool in softening their visual impact is to plant up the vertical structures. Above all you should rely on your imagination when designing boundaries because they can transform an entire garden.

15 ways to... buff up your boundaries

1. Try out colour effects

When used on boundaries hot or bright colours will emphasize them and make the space look smaller. Cool or dark colours will visually enhance the size of the coloured area because they appear ambiguous and ill-defined.

3. Establish unity

A single boundary style around the whole garden contributes to a sense of unity and ensures that the focus is on the features within the garden itself rather than on the boundary.

4. Check fence ownership

Generally you will own the right-hand boundary as you look into the garden, and your neighbour will own the left-hand one. Check ownership details on your property deeds. It is conventional to have the framework side of a boundary fence that you own facing your garden, and the other, more attractive side should be displayed toward your neighbour's garden.

5. Avoid disputes

Some boundaries may be formed by buildings with damp-proof courses that must not be breached by any changes of level in your garden. You should not attach anything to these walls without the owner's permission, nor excavate close by.

7. Camouflage boundaries

Climbers provide a good space-saving option for hiding boundaries. Check how your selected climbing plant grows (see p113). Some, such as *Hydrangea anomala* subsp. *petiolaris*, use suckers to attach to walls and brickwork, but can be less successful when trained against timber fences.

2. Make room for wildlife

When designing a boundary you may want to consider wildlife access to your garden and whether the boundary will provide a useful habitat. Hedges composed of diverse native species are the best local habitat because they may well replace those removed in the last 50 years by farmers.

6. Unite different materials

If you have a number of different fence types in your garden co-ordinate them with a wood stain. Black or dark green stains will reduce the impact of the boundaries and will instead emphasize your planting scheme.

8. Consider hedge problems

Typically hedges are 0.75–1m (2¹/₂–3ft) wide so may occupy too much space in a small garden. Maintenance from within the garden is straightforward, but think about the outer face of the hedge and how this will be looked after. In small gardens there is little room for an additional maintenance area in order to access both sides. Potentially you may therefore be expecting your neighbour to maintain their side, which they may not altogether welcome.

9. Pleach for privacy

Where privacy or high-level screening is important pleached hedges may offer a successful planted solution.

10. Train plants

Some climbers such as ivy (Hedera) grip the wall itself using aerial roots. Others such as clematis climb using tendrils and need trellis or wired supports. Fix the trellis onto supports that allow space between it and the wall, enabling the plants to twine through. Vine eyes can be used to keep training wires away from the wall. Tie wall shrubs or train fruit trees (see above) to these supports, thereby making use of otherwise bare walls.

Specialist nurseries will supply these clipped hedges already pruned into shape on clear trunks. As with any hedge, consider the way in which you will maintain and access this form of hedging plant.

11. Erect fences

Fences occupy less space than walls and are appropriate in situations where mature planting exists. Supporting posts need individual foundations, which can be spaced between existing roots, rather than the continuous strip foundation below ground needed for walls.

12. Build walls

Walls last longer than fences but cost more. They offer an extra level of privacy from sights and sounds of neighbours and the world outside.

13. Plant living boundaries

The recent advance in vertical planting techniques means that boundary structures can be green and organic although they still rely on a constructed framework.

14. Erect balustrades

If you are designing a roof garden you need to include a balustrade for safety. The required height is 1.1m (43in) above the finished level of the roof garden. Also check with a structural engineer on the suitability of the roof for garden conversion (see pp26–27).

15. Check regulations

If you live in a listed building or a conservation area, there may be legal restrictions in force about the specific materials, heights and finishes to your garden boundaries and in some cases to planting too. Always check with your local authority on such issues.

Boundary basics

How you define the extent of your garden depends on whether it has existing boundaries or is a new-build property where the boundary markers have not yet been erected.

New developments

Before you move in it is a good idea to discuss types of garden boundary with your developer, to ensure that they do not erect cheap and flimsy panels that will struggle to endure the first storms of winter. As these are usually installed at a height of 1m (3ft) they also provide little privacy. Instead request

▼ **Distressed wall finishes** can add depth to small spaces owing to the variations in colour. Here ivy (*Hedera helix*) adds to the effect.

close-board (see p116) or hit-and-miss fencing (see p117) erected to a height of 1.8m (6ft).

Existing walls

These should be carefully assessed for subsidence or root damage, which can undermine foundations or even push walls over. Brick walls that are sufficiently high to give privacy should be two bricks thick. Such a solid structure however can still be pushed over by strong winds in more exposed situations. If necessary reinforce the wall or add brick piers for additional strength.

Where a shared boundary is in a poor state of repair but is owned by your neighbour it may be worth offering to pay for a new boundary in order to secure your garden and create the necessary privacy or visual unity. Alternatively, and if space allows, you could erect a fence or trellis screen immediately in front of the boundary in order to produce a more consistent result.

If you wish to introduce walls into a garden that has mature vegetation and root networks close to the boundaries, it is possible to include a lintel within the wall structure that will span the major roots to prevent damage from foundation excavations.

Existing fences

Check the condition of the timber in all fencing. Wood in contact with the ground will often rot first, weakening the structure and reducing security. If the main timber supports are set into the ground these can be the main

weak points. A barge board along the length of timber panels can reduce damage to individual fence boards and also minimize weed infestation from adjacent properties.

Barge boards can also be fitted to trellis panels, which make perfectly workable boundaries, while increasing light penetration into the garden and providing plant support for climbers. Many bespoke trellis systems are decoratively patterned or have smaller openings or gaps to improve privacy.

▶ **A natural stone wall** plays host to sedums, lichens and tiny ferns making homes in the joints and crevices. Facing stone can play a similar role.

These boundaries mix architecture and planters with hornbeam columns to screen and soften. Low-level seating adds to privacy.

Boundary materials

Traditionally garden boundaries were constructed in brick or timber with occasional use of stone if that was a local material.

Wooden fences

Timber is often favoured because it is cheap, easy to work and quick to install, but it does need concrete foundations. Wood often needs regular maintenance to prolong its life. Most timber used for fences is pressure-treated softwood although higher-cost hardwoods will have a longer life span. Wood will eventually rot when in contact with ground dampness. However early rotting can be minimized if timber posts are held above soil in spiked steel supports driven into the ground. Concrete foundations may not then be required.

All wood used for fences and trellises should be certified by a relevant timber authority, ensuring that it has been sourced from well-managed woodland.

Styles of fencing

Most fences comprise vertical posts with two or three horizontal rails connecting the various posts together. Timber planks are nailed or screwed vertically onto these rails to produce the fence itself.

In close-board fencing the vertical timber planks may overlap, butt together or be fixed with narrow gaps between each plank. Typically the distance between the main supporting posts is 1.8–2.4m (6–8ft) and is based on the thickness of the rails and posts chosen.

Slatted timber fences have a similar framework to close-board fencing but the added timber comprises narrow 50mm (2in) wide wooden strips

Boundaries play an important part in the composition of Japanese gardens while intricate bamboo patterns and fixings enhance their essential character.

laid horizontally with narrow gaps between each strip. This gives a more contemporary and stylish appearance with a horizontal emphasis that works well in contrast to the organic nature of planting.

In hit-and-miss fences the timber planks are fixed alternately on both sides of a supporting frame with open gaps between. This style is always worth considering if you have agreed to renew a shared boundary, as both parties will achieve the same look. By angling individual posts or timbers along a fence line you can enjoy views through the boundary in one direction while maintaining a degree of privacy. Light can also penetrate into the garden in this way, reducing the impact of shade.

Trellis fencing

Trellis is another good solution for shade reduction. Most trellis is available in preconstructed panels although some manufacturers will fit bespoke designs. Use the most sturdy trellis you can, as wind and planting weight can damage lightweight panels.

CHOOSING A WOODEN FENCE

1. **Woven hurdles** in hazel or willow provide organic screens and boundary fence panels that support climbers with their open weave.

2. **This vertically woven panel** of oak strips establishes a rhythmically patterned, semitransparent boundary.

3. **Split bamboo** creates a textured screen that glows with light and glimmers with the colours of the glimpsed view beyond.

4. **Close-board fences**, normally of softwood, can be stained for protection and for colour co-ordination with the rest of the garden.

Garden walls

If you build a wall around your garden use an expansion joint at the point where the house and garden wall meet or if you need a gate use the gate opening to keep the structures apart. Do not attach the garden wall to your house because the two structures will heat and cool in different ways and will expand and contract at different rates as a result.

Unsightly walls can be covered by slats fixed to horizontal timber battens mounted on the wall surface. A range of plank or slat sizes is available and these can be mixed for a random look.

Brick walls

Brick is the traditional material for garden walls and produces a solid,

secure and long-lasting structure. Such walls are supported by concrete foundations in trenches below ground.

The bricks should match as closely as possible those used in the property or in the locality. London, for example, is famed for its buff/yellow bricks. Often cheaper bricks known as 'commons' are used below ground level while the more expensive bricks show above the ground. In some cases concrete blocks are laid below ground.

Damp protection

Walls are prone to moisture damage in two directions: below and above. To prevent damp in the soil rising through the wall and weakening it, include a damp-proof course just above ground level. This can be a manufactured strip, engineering bricks or slate.

The top of a wall can also be penetrated by rain unless it is protected by 'coping'. Special coping materials are available or engineering bricks can be used as a feature. Some copings are wider than the wall to allow the water to drip clear of it. Tiles and slates are useful additional weatherproofing materials for a wall.

Brick walls built without such damp-proofing measures will become stained as the water penetrates. Although this will give an aged look, with mosses and lichens growing on the surface, the life of the wall will be reduced. Frost action can also damage the wall and its structure.

Brick patterns

Bricks have a bed face, an edge and an end. In most walls bricks are laid

DIY DESIGN

Sound in a small garden

- In urban gardens, sound pollution is a major issue because solid boundaries such as walls reduce or deflect more sound than planted boundaries or fences.
- Boundaries that are insulated for sound are available but use more space than standard walls and fences.
- Use sound within the garden as a distraction. Moving water, such as splashing jets or cascades, does this in pools, onto drained paved surfaces or against walls.
- Plants such as bamboos, birch (*Betula*) or aspen (*Populus*) rustle and whisper in the breeze. Most tall ornamental grasses also add sound as the wind blows through them.

Second-hand or rescued brick has been used in this solid boundary wall full of colour variations, which are picked up by the weathered decking. Coping bricks on edge and a tile overhang prolong the life of the wall.

The dark rendered walls of this small space recede visually to allow the planting and lighter paving to take centre stage.

on their bed face and in some form of interlocking pattern to provide additional strength to the wall. Coping bricks can be laid on edge so that a denser layer of brickwork sheds water more successfully.

The dimensions of bricks means that they will fit together neatly when laid with a 10mm (1/2in) mortar joint between each brick and between each course (or row).

The most common brick pattern is known as stretcher bond. Others such as Flemish bond and English garden wall bond are variations on this theme. On your garden wall it is a good idea to match the brick pattern of your property walls or those used locally.

Rendered walls

For a contemporary look add an external render to the wall and then paint the smooth surface. Normally such a wall is constructed with concrete blocks to which the render is applied. Alternatively you can colour the render itself with natural pigments. Such self-coloured render will last without the need to repaint.

 This sun-drenched terra-cotta rendered wall suggesting searing heat contrasts well with the spearlike leaves of *Agave americana*.

Beading is included at the wall corners to define the edges and at the base of the wall to prevent the render coming into contact with the ground.

Waterproof renders can be used on the top of the wall, although a coping stone will also help to shed water off the structure.

Stone walls

Stone walls tend to be a thing of the past as solid structures, because the material is expensive and often requires skilled labour. Both sides of boundary walls should be dressed – the outer side being visible to your neighbour. Stone is now most likely to be used as a decorative facing on concrete-block walls, and this form of construction is most likely to be found on screening or decorative walls within the garden. A mix of smooth rendered boundary walls and textured stone screen walls within the garden would generate a strong visual contrast.

Boundary plants

Plants can be used successfully to define the limits of your garden. However planting occupies more space than a wall or fence – with a hedge often growing 1m (3ft) or more deep – and this may not be suitable in a small garden. Tall hedges can shield more private spaces than lower ones, but they also increase shade levels, absorb more nutrients and moisture from the soil and potentially cause nuisance for your neighbours. There is no statutory height for boundary hedges (unlike constructed features such as walls). Many owners need secure boundaries, and most planted boundaries do not meet this criteria.

Hedge wars

The fashion for planting fast-growing x *Cuprocyparis leylandii* hedges in the late-20th century backfired on many gardeners as the ability of this species to grow outran the owner's ability to keep up with its maintenance. This triggered many disputes with adjacent property owners whose gardens or houses were overshadowed by incredibly tall and dense boundary hedges. Mature hedges of this species do not respond well to drastic pruning. Some countries have introduced legislation to restrict the planting of this hedge or to ease its removal.

Climbing plants

Climbers are particularly useful for softening boundaries and generating a sense of unity especially when a single species has been planted several times within a small garden. Some climbers such as evergreen *Clematis armandii* tolerate a certain amount of shade, provide fragrant clouds of cream flowers and have long willowlike leaves to green up your walls or trellis all-year-round. When designing your planting scheme, consider such hardworking characteristics as well as the coherence each plant will offer to your plot. Against a soft but consistent

Here brick walls create a private courtyard feeling with a good sound barrier and visual screening. Climbers, varied planting and water are used to soften the wall.

◀ **Clipped yew hedges,** distracting the eye from the house and boundaries, create screens and spaces within the garden.

boundary backdrop other planting can then be introduced.

Vertical planting

Since the early 2000s it has been fashionable to add planting onto the vertical surfaces of buildings and walls. The French designer Patrick Blanc has been instrumental in developing this concept, which works well in small gardens. A range of systems is used to incorporate pouches, pockets or troughs that are planted and irrigated. The planting system is fixed to a solid structure.

The walls can be used productively with herbs, tomatoes, soft fruits and salad crops or as a purely decorative feature. The higher planting positions tend to favour sun-loving species that tolerate drier conditions, while the lower planting ones are more suitable for moisture- or shade-lovers.

More ambitious systems can be used on the façades of houses and apartments. In these the air between the framework and the walls acts as an invaluable insulating layer.

Planting beside boundaries

The massing of plants in front of a boundary can effectively disguise the boundary itself (see p44). A sense of ambiguity is generated, as is a perception that the garden is larger in scale. Where space is tight a single large bed with a good depth and scale of planting is much more worthwhile than a series of smaller beds around the garden, which will serve only to make the area look limited and bitty. Always use bold planting with vertical emphasis or interesting architectural forms in order to distract the eye.

DIY DESIGN

Layering a climber to cover a wall

Climbers offer an easy way to green a wall or boundary, but most climbers tend to grow straight up the surface.
- Fan shoots out when planting to ensure that the wall surface will covered by a good spread of vegetation.
- Pull selected shoots down to soil level and secure in position with a metal peg or stone. Leave this weighted shoot for a period of time to allow roots to form. Either allow the new plant to broaden the spread of the original or sever the rooted shoots from the parent and plant them elsewhere.
- Many climbers such as ivy or climbing hydrangea have trailing shoots that root naturally when in contact with the soil. Leave these *in situ* or sever as appropriate.

Plants trained vertically up boundary walls and screens visually soften their supports, increase the ground space available for functional use and introduce greater plant diversity.

A sense of depth and visual interest has been established by positioning a pergola away from the boundary wall so it screens the wall itself and enhances privacy with its height and choice of planting.

BOUNDARIES: CASE STUDY

HARDWORKING BOUNDARIES

In this courtyard garden to a terraced house in southwest London, designer Maria Örnberg has used planting for the backdrop to the main garden space.

The raised beds lift the planting away from the clean-lined space in the centre, which is flexible enough for relaxation or outdoor entertaining.

The planting palette is designed to emphasize foliage textures, such as those of the tall, elegant *Miscanthus sinensis* 'Silberfeder' with the tighter mounded forms of euphorbia. Meanwhile the dramatic lime-tinged flowers of *Hydrangea paniculata* 'Limelight' provide an eye-catching seasonal highlight.

At the far end of the garden, tall pleached hornbeams *(Carpinus betulus)* provide an alternative green screen to the trellis that runs around the garden boundaries. Taller fencing might be restricted by planning legislation. Consider the maintenance implications of pleached trees as access to the outer face of the hedge might be difficult.

Design ideas to take home

- Planting softens and screens the existing boundaries.
- Privacy enhanced by taller plants including pleached hornbeam.
- Neutral-coloured grey reduces the impact of the garden walls and establishes consistent colour and material.
- Floor space has been maximized for a flexible entertaining or functional space within the garden.
- Choice of a single paving material focuses attention on the planting.

An extended room

The rear wall of the house opens up into the garden so there is a single entertaining space, which would be ideal for summer. The area can be further enhanced by decorative lighting for evenings, while items of architectural interest or use can easily be dropped into this space to create focal points of interest.

▶ **A single space** for more ambitious entertaining has been achieved by opening up the bifold doors in the back wall of this house. By appearing to bring the garden indoors, the boundary between interior and garden has been blurred.

... simplicity
and privacy
are key in
this elegant,
relaxing
courtyard...

COOL AND NEUTRAL

In this flexible and usable but very confined space most of the emphasis has been placed on the boundary treatment.

A pleached hedge (1) of hornbeam provides soft visual screening at height to enclose the garden, hiding nearby properties.

Trellis (2) has been erected on the side boundaries so the climbers can soften their support as well as conceal adjacent properties.

The walls, trellis and planting bed are painted in the same shade of grey (3).

The simple planting combination of box (*Buxus*) (4), feathery *Miscanthus sinensis* 'Silberfeder', calamagrostis and *Hydrangea paniculata* 'Limelight' – echoed in the sulphur-yellow, early flowerheads of spurge (*Euphorbia*) – bring light and movement into the space.

A gentle trickle from the wall-mounted water fountain (5) introduces sound into the garden and helps disguise the background noise of the city.

◀ **Decorative details such as** this glazed candle lantern not only supplement the basic theme of the garden but also provide welcome atmospheric lighting.

SMALL GARDEN

STRUCTURES

Garden structures may be purely functional or more decorative and indulgent, but when space is tight these buildings have to perform several functions.

Storage cupboards or sheds are essential for garden tools, furniture and barbecues – and bicycles or pots may need shelter too. As more waste is recycled, convenient storage space may need to be allocated. It should be close to hand, yet fit well into the garden's ethos.

Pergolas and arbours offer shade, an escape and a site for vertical planting, while garden offices can take pressure off space in your home. Position gazebos or summerhouses so they form focal points within the garden.

15 ways to... use garden structures

4. Try slim storage

A variety of storage solutions are available for gardens that are very restricted on space. A narrow cupboard or half-height shed for example can be slotted into a narrow access passage, against a garden wall or behind an area of decorative planting.

can be utilized for storage. Such a storage space must be waterproofed. Access from within the deck can be provided by trapdoor.

5. Find new growing areas

All surfaces within the garden present planting opportunities. Use windowsills, the tops of storage units or refuse bin stores for salad crops or herbs. Even vertical wall surfaces can now be planted.

6. Keep pergolas in scale

These structures should be carefully considered as part of the overall garden design. Make the scale bold and assertive, and ensure that the pergola is high enough to support

1. Camouflage sheds

Traditionally the garden shed accommodates most outdoor storage needs. Built in softwood, they are serviceable but utilitarian. By staining these structures in black or dark green they will recede and appear smaller. Planting or trellis can be used to disguise or screen these structures. A mono-pitch roof will often be lower in height.

2. Attach cupboards

Use the vertical surfaces in your garden to support storage areas. Storage cupboards can be fixed to house walls as built-in units in order to save space. Use slatted timber for an architectural quality.

3. Raise decking

If a timber deck is raised above ground level on a platform, the space beneath climbers while allowing you to walk freely below. Many off-the-peg pergolas are flimsily built and out of scale with most gardens.

7. Use pergolas in different ways

Although many pergolas are designed to support climbing plants, others are more suitable as shading or framing structures, such as around an outdoor dining area. Blinds or curtains can be incorporated to increase shade and privacy. In some cases these filters can be automated.

8. Check arch positioning

Arches or other structures to frame views can be effective in small spaces, as they can provide a strong focus to a path or entrance. Make sure that they are sufficiently bold in scale and proportion in order to catch the eye.

9. Erect a glasshouse

A wide variety of glasshouses ideal for small spaces is now available. Some provide a structure supported by boundary or house walls, effectively covering half the space of a freestanding glasshouse. Others

stand on a turntable base, allowing plants to be turned towards the light. For permanent siting, ensure the orientation is correct (see p135).

10. Consider a garden office

As working patterns become increasingly flexible, the concept of working from home and creating an office in the garden is growing in popularity. Ensure that the size of your building meets local planning guidelines and that it is sufficiently insulated for year-round use.

11. Add a conservatory

Conservatories and other garden rooms are light-filled spaces in which you can enjoy the garden even in bad weather. These structures can be freestanding or attached to the house but must conform to local planning rules and be well ventilated. Conservatories can overheat in summer, and condensation can be a problem in colder weather.

12. Exploit green roofs

For garden buildings with a solid roof such as sheds and summerhouses the addition of a green roof can increase

13. Design an arbour

Erect an arbour instead of a larger summerhouse if you want a sheltered retreat in a garden where space is already tight. This may be little more than a covered or recessed bench that can double up as an architectural focal point.

biodiversity within the garden and absorb rainwater. Use sedum matting to convert such roofs. New structures can be designed from the outset to take more varied planting on the roof.

14. Build raised beds

By lifting the planting surface off the ground the effect of shade can be reduced and planting is easily reached. Each raised planting bed should be built over soil, not a hard surface, so plants can drain freely and access moisture from the ground below.

15. Construct a gazebo

Gazebo structures are meant to be open and transparent, creating a focal point within the garden as well as a frame from which the best views can be enjoyed. Their light and open character means they do not dominate a small space.

Storage

For most gardeners the need for storage space is met by the erection of a shed. However even a small shed will dominate a small garden, where it is often difficult to disguise such structures. Try to be consistent in the way in which these structures are constructed and finished. Think about and plan all your storage needs as you first begin to plan the garden.

What do you want to store?

The frequency of use and the kind of storage you require affect your choice of structure and its size. Bicycle and barbecue storage for example requires a different approach to the need for an area in which to keep a few tools and pots. If you have a young family then storage for toys and bikes may be paramount, but this priority may alter as the children become older.

The traditional shed is a low-cost structure made from pressure-treated

softwood. It should sit on a prepared base, created as a foundation to reduce damp and increase the lifespan of the timber. There are many variations on the basic design with some including one or more windows and shelving or a potting bench.

▲ **Water butts can be concealed** by trellis or slatted timber panels to reduce their visual impact on the garden.

Shed variations

Typically a small garden shed will be 1.2m (4ft) wide and 1.8m (6ft) long.

DIY DESIGN

Minimizing the impact of storage

- Use pot-grown or other plants to distract attention from unsightly sheds, bins, compost heaps and water butts.
- Trellis panels are ideal in a small garden as they take up little space on the ground.
- For additional cover choose climbers such as clematis and ivy that twine or support themselves with tendrils.
- Paint timber sheds, garden trellis and other storage structures with black, dark grey, dark green and dark blue stain to reduce the apparent size and mass of these structures and to allow planting to dominate the garden and catch the eye. Stains can also protect and prolong the life of timber, which is an easy way to lower costs long-term.

▶ **The top of this cupboard** for storing tools has been cleverly used to grow salad leaves. In a small garden every square metre counts.

If space permits it can be screened in some way, perhaps by climbers and trellis. Instead of a ridged roof, a flat or mono-pitch one may be more appropriate as the overall height of the shed will be reduced. Flat or mono-pitch roofs also work well as green roofs, which will soften the structure and so can also reduce the overall impact of the building. By adding a dark stain to the timber you can minimize the mass and silhouette of the shed, especially if you combine this with planting in front of or up the shed.

Room for a glasshouse?

Sheds generally provide poor growing conditions, because light levels are too low. The decision to expand into a glasshouse, where light is considerably better, relies not only on your gardening skills and time commitment to plant care but also on the amount of space you have. However glasshouses make poor storage areas. A smaller version of a glasshouse or of a shed may be the most appropriate solution.

For the smallest gardens

For really small or restricted spaces, wall-supported structures and outdoor cupboards may provide better storage facilities. Side passages and access ways may be suitable places for these as well as for refuse or recycling bins, thereby reducing the level of clutter in the rear or front gardens. However larger items such as bicycles and barbecues are unlikely to fit in them.

Glasshouses & other frames

A glasshouse, cold frame or polytunnel is a useful facility for extending the growing season and enabling new crops to be propagated or nurtured before seasonal temperatures rise sufficiently for unprotected planting.

The importance of orientation

A main purpose of a glasshouse is to maximize light, and in this respect the orientation of the structure is an essential design consideration that may present difficulties in a small garden, where there may be few or no places for it to be sited optimally.

The most popular shape for a glasshouse is rectangular. Domed, pyramidal and revolving cylindrical structures are also available and designed to maximize light levels.

Before purchasing a glasshouse of any type it is essential to find out the orientation of your garden. A north-facing garden may well be in shade for much of the year depending on the height of the house, any surrounding boundaries or overhanging trees. In this case it is unlikely that crops or propagation would be possible either in a glasshouse or in the wider garden – most vegetables, all fruits, salads and herbs needing high levels of sunshine to succeed.

In sunnier or lighter gardens, a ridged glasshouse is ideally positioned on an east–west axis or as close to this orientation as possible. Here it will maximize early spring light, which is vital for new plants. However later in the season the glasshouse will overheat, as sunlight levels and day lengths increase. You then need to ventilate and shade it. If you are using the glasshouse in the winter months, it may need artificial heating.

Timber or metal frame?

Galvanized steel or aluminium-framed glasshouses allow more light to penetrate, as the glazing bars are narrower than those held within a timber structure. However these metals will affect the appearance of the glasshouse; you may prefer the softer look of wood.

Other glasshouse features

If possible prepare some planting beds within the glasshouse in which larger, more tender plants can be overwintered. This will increase the diversity and range of plants in your garden as a whole.

Surfaces around the glasshouse should be paved so that you can work around the structure and move plants and tools easily. Such hardscaping might be a good surface on which to position a cold frame, which is useful for hardening off plants as well as overwintering them.

For the smallest plots

Smaller glasshouses can be invaluable, and it may be possible to use the house façade or a tall boundary wall to support a lean-to glasshouse. However the most important consideration is the orientation of the proposed glasshouse rather than its shape. Otherwise use cold frames or small polytunnels for plant protection.

◀ **A potting bench** will provide an invaluable workspace, so try to accommodate even a modest one in your shed or glasshouse.

... a glasshouse helps extend the season and your range of crops...

Correct glasshouse orientation is vital for crops if they are to get enough light to thrive. The frame should lie on an east–west axis (or as close to it as possible).

Raised beds

Raised beds can be appropriate for shaded gardens and for children and less-abled users. By raising the growing surface, light levels can improve, resulting in enhanced growth and productivity, as well as easier access. Less bending is also required when caring for the crops. Soil in raised beds warms up quickly, which should raise yields. The ample depth is also excellent for root crops.

Size of the beds

Although larger beds will naturally hold more moisture, it is important to consider overall size in relation to reach. For gardeners in a wheelchair, the height of the raised bed should be considered from a seated position. A height of 60–75cm (24–30in) and width of 1.2m (4ft) are most workable.

Keep the bases of raised beds in contact with the soil below, as this improves drainage and allows deep-rooting plants to access ground water. Despite this, raised beds dry out faster than ground-level ones, so dig in plenty of humus to increase their moisture-holding capacity.

Paths around a raised bed

As part of the design, think about the paths surrounding each raised bed. Wheelchair users need level paths 1m (3ft) wide, which should also be wide enough for a wheelbarrow.

Raised beds in a small garden can affect the perceived space, making the garden seem claustrophobic. By keeping the height of planters low and paths wide, this visual conundrum can be resolved.

◀ **Raised beds are convenient** for easy access and maintenance. Both planter and path-width dimensions should be as generous as possible.

A **conservatory forms** a bridge between the house and garden. Use it to overwinter tender or exotic plants from the garden.

Garden rooms

Conservatories and other glazed structures can extend the length of time that you enjoy your garden. They can also push interior spaces out into the garden and diffuse the boundary.

Differing requirements

When planning such an all-weather garden room, the most important decision is who will have priority – plants or humans – because a shared environment will not suit both.

To use these garden rooms primarily for planting you need careful temperature and humidity control as well as protection from the pests that can flourish in these environments. Ventilation, shading from the higher light levels in summer and orientation must all be considered in addition to the choice of appropriate plants.

To make a garden room comfortable for humans, planting would have to be reduced to just a few decorative specimens that will survive in the conditions that humans prefer.

Planning permission

If you are adding a conservatory or other glazed structure to your house the extension would normally fall under what is known as 'permitted development' and would not require planning permission. However such a structure must not occupy more than a certain proportion of the available garden space – a consideration especially pertinent to small gardens.

There are also many restrictions on the overall height of the conservatory structure, its roof detailing and the choice of materials.

For those living in apartments or maisonettes, planning permission will be required for any alteration and extension to the buildings.

Listed buildings

If you live in a listed building you will have to apply for permission to change or extend the building in any way. In general nothing can be attached to your listed building without prior permission. Your local authority on their website should publish information concerning the specific details of what is or is not permitted.

Summerhouses & hideaways

A summerhouse can be incorporated into your design as a focal point and as a place in which to escape. Although this may seem a luxury, it is often beneficial to withdraw from the pressures of modern life to enjoy stolen moments of relaxation.

A summerhouse with space to dine for two, or perhaps four, offers shade from the hot sun and a shelter from those heavy but atmospheric cloudbursts of high summer.

Although these structures can be used as covered workspaces, this can be for no more than an occasional or informal use because of their lack of proper insulation.

Selection of materials

When deciding on a structure, ensure its scale is appropriate and that it uses the materials identified in your chosen palette for the whole garden.

Other considerations

Think about orientation for shade and for privacy. Use of the summerhouse can be extended to well after dark if you install lighting – making it an ideal place to wind down.

▼ **Because it has slatted sides**, the air flows through this building so it is a cool haven on warm evenings. The raised deck offers a vantage point and expands the usable space.

... a place to enjoy a few stolen moments of relaxation...

The back of this green-roofed structure comprises sawn logs, which make a great home for small insects. These are a food source for birds.

Garden offices

The use of the garden as a working environment is gaining in popularity, as it offers a tranquil and inspirational environment in which to work. The division of house and workplace is important for many people, and even though this separation may be only a few paces down the garden this can be enough to create a more productive working environment.

Some companies specialize in the construction of bespoke offices that can be imported into the garden complete with planning approval. Make sure that the building you require can be accommodated into the garden in terms of its finishes and general styling.

Basic comfort

Insulation is the most important consideration for the building you will be spending an extended time in, in all seasons, so it needs to be warm in winter and cool in summer.

Good insulation will also allow you to store paperwork and electrical equipment without the worry of condensation and the damage it can cause. You also need to research what lighting best suits your needs.

Office utilities

It is important also to think about the routing of telephone lines and the electricity supply, although with mobile telephones and wi-fi access it may be possible to work near the house without a separate connection.

After careful consideration of the amount of space and light you need, look carefully at what is permitted by your local planning authority.

▼ **Garden offices need to** be insulated in order to maintain a workable temperature in both summer and winter.

... your workplace may be a few paces down the garden...

Check with your local planning authority on its guidelines for the erection of new garden buildings. Any regulations will relate to the height and overall size.

Planning guidelines for offices, sheds and storage facilities

In many countries there are important planning guidelines for garden storage or decorative structures such as garden offices. These are aimed at maintaining open space in the garden and good neighbour relations.

In general, sheds and other structures are not allowed in front garden spaces, which are subject to greater planning control. Buildings will not be allowed between the road and the house façade, and no structure should be located closer than 20m (60ft) from the highway.

A shed will not necessarily require planning permission, but it should occupy no more than 50 percent of the overall floor space available in any garden. For a flat or mono-pitch roof the maximum height allowable is 3m (10ft) and for a ridged-roof shed the maximum height is 4m (13ft) along the ridge.

If you live within a conservation area you may find that there are further restrictions on the size of your garden building. A maximum of 10 cu m (353 cu ft) is allowed before planning permission is required.

Opportunities for green roofs

Any redevelopment of your garden by the erection of new buildings and other structures will produce additional roof surfaces, which need careful thought, because the extra rainwater runoff from any new roofs will put additional pressure on the wider drainage system for your locality.

While it is possible to capture and store runoff water in water butts attached to downpipes it is likely that a large amount of roof water will be lost.

Softening impact

Green roof systems provide a range of advantages in the garden. They are a planting opportunity on the surface area of each roof structure. Aesthetically this can soften and reduce the impact of a building, in some way helping to unify the structure with the surrounding landscape.

The plants absorb rainwater, using a proportion of the rainfall to support plant growth. Their growing medium will also absorb water and slow down its release into the general drainage system. This can prevent catastrophic flooding, especially on a wider community basis.

Pitched roof planting

Although often used with flat or mono-pitch roofs, it is possible to add plants to a sloping or ridged roof.

Preplanted mats can be secured to an existing roof. They generally contain sedums, as these shallow-rooting plants are tolerant of drought.

When planning a new building, the planting depth on the roof can

▶ **This green roof significantly** increases the diversity for flora and fauna, and divides the garden spaces effectively. It softens the impact of a garden shed too.

be increased to accommodate meadow plants and a wider mix of perennials. However by restricting your roof planting to low-growing perennials and grasses, the depth of soil can be minimized to retain an elegant proportion in the roof design of your garden building.

Extra biodiversity

The increase in species diversity, especially as a feeding resource for insects and invertebrates, will expand the wildlife value of the garden on what would otherwise be an arid, sterile and heat-reflective surface.

DIY DESIGN

Choice of roof plants

- Always seek professional advice on the strength of the roof structure before doing any planting.
- Traditionally sedums can be planted in shallow mats to green an existing rooftop.
- Other species of perennials and grasses that require only shallow soils of 10–15cm (4–6in) include thyme (*Thymus*), stachys, *Stipa tenuissima*, blue fescue (*Festuca glauca*), chives (*Allium schoenoprasum*) and yellow *Sisyrinchium striatum* (shown, right). These species provide a good variety of height and form, and they work beside lower sedums, saxifages and sempervivums to create a rich and varied tapestry on green roofs with their specialized conditions.

… green roofs broaden the wildlife value of the garden…

STRUCTURES:
CASE STUDY

CREATING PRIVACY & DEPTH

The generous path width in this small garden, designed by Robin Williams, allows the space beneath the pergola to be used for seating or outdoor dining.

Brick is used as the common material in the pergola, boundary walls and repeated as a detail in the paving elsewhere in the garden. Combined with the scale of the pergola in both width and height there is a consistency and strength in this small garden.

The side borders are generously filled with tall and dense planting, while the composition is completed by a mirrored recess, bringing light and additional depth to the space.

Opportunities for planting

Part of the illusion in using mirrors is to continue them down to ground level. This tricks the eye into thinking that the scene runs on indefinitely, thus expanding the garden. If the edges of the mirror are not visible, the eye is more easily deceived.

▲ **Water flowing from a small spout** to a bowl below makes a welcoming, distracting sound.

▼ **A seat or bench recessed** into a planting bed leaves the main paved space looking uncluttered and more usable.

4

Design ideas to take home

- Structures within the garden can create privacy and shelter.
- Pergolas especially are useful to screen overlooking buildings and windows.
- The scale of the structure must work well, as here, and allow space for planting beneath.
- Pergolas can be left bare of climbers; this improves light penetration to plants below.

... magical
reflections
deceive the eye
and expand the
narrow space...

PRIVATE RETREAT

The pergola (1) spans the entire garden, maintaining a good sense of scale and providing support for a range of climbers that will add both shade and colour over the year.

Warm-toned brick is used throughout the main structural elements of this small garden such as the rear wall (2), which disguises a small storage shed.

The brick arch is infilled with a mirror (3). This focal point of the garden creates the illusion of greater depth and a space beyond.

Generously planted borders (4) soften the impact of such an enclosed space.

◀ **French windows open outwards** to link indoors and out. Brick in the raised bed and paving detail echoes that in the house walls.

SMALL GARDEN

WATER

Water is a natural material that interacts with the local environment. It transforms a garden by introducing sound, light reflection and movement. It energizes and refreshes the atmosphere, and it can soften and mask background noise. Such a mercurial material is capable of changing its character and mood in the blink of an eye and is notorious for finding its own equilibrium.

Uniquely, water can be forced, aerated, cascaded, stilled or disturbed to produce a range of effects. Surely it is an essential component of any small urban garden.

15 ways to... enjoy water

1. Establish the correct depth

The depth of a garden pond is critical. If it is too shallow, the water overheats, leading to algal bloom and evaporation; if too deep, there will be excessive spoil, which in a small garden is difficult to absorb. A water depth of 70–100cm (28–36in) is fine. It allows lower levels to remain cool, and balances the heat of the upper levels.

2. Containing water

In most gardens water will be artificially introduced rather than a naturally occurring element. As such it must be contained in some way to prevent leakage and loss. This can be done with a flexible material such as butyl rubber to form a natural, organic shape or with more rigid materials such as fibreglass or concrete for a precise architectural character.

3. Selecting a site

Pools of water in full sun will be energized and potentially full of life, but they can overheat readily. Those sited in shade will be lifeless and dank. In heavy shade consider alternative approaches such as jets, which rely on water stored beneath the surface.

4. Moving water

Install pumps to move and aerate water. This can reduce or moderate a rise in water temperature within the feature and helps water to stay fresh, thus preventing the build-up of algal growth. The sound and movement are added attractions.

5. Installing a pump

Pumps can be submerged within the water, especially in a small feature, which requires only an electrical connection. More sophisticated

6. Co-ordinating the design

One of the greatest challenges when designing a garden is to establish a satisfactory connection between artificially contained water and the surrounding dry land. The edges of rigid pools, ponds and other water features can fairly readily be concealed or disguised by paving or other hard materials. In planted pools the liner can be extended out into the garden area, but unless well covered with plants it can easily be on show or prone to damage there.

or complex water features may have pumps installed away from the water and so need access for maintenance.

7. Storing underground

Water stored in an underground tank will have a lower temperature than when exposed to sunlight. Such concealed facilities work well for cascades or jets that might emerge from walls or paving, draining back into the reservoir. They also utilize space efficiently.

8. Producing reflections

The internal walls or liners in a pool should be black or as dark as possible to create a mirrorlike surface that will shimmer with reflection and light.

9. Balancing the ecosystem

It is possible to plant ponds and pools and to treat the water as a living ecosystem. Although it may take some time to balance the different components, such pools will dramatically increase biodiversity within your garden.

10. Illuminating water

Highlight surfaces or planting on the far side of your pool or pond, so that after dark they will be reflected on the surface of the water. Do not be tempted to include lights within the pool itself, as this will reveal the silt, wiring and pumps.

11. Treating water

If you require the water to be clear in your pool, it will probably have to be treated chemically, in order to prevent algal growth. Ultraviolet filters also deter algae. Clear pools need regular upkeep and are treated more like swimming pools.

12. Topping up with rainwater

Refill or top up your pond with rainwater rather than mains water, because the latter is high in nutrient and feeds green algae. Introducing nutrients will counteract any aim of balancing the ecosystem.

13. Including depth variations

Most aquatic and marginal plants require specific water depths in order to flourish. Suitable raised and deeper areas, shelves and beaches for emerging wildlife should therefore be incorporated into the pool design.

14. Addressing safety issues

Many people worry about the safety of children when there is water in the garden. However, by taking the necessary precautions and by educating children about its risks, you can include water in your design in such a way that children can enjoy the benefits it can bring.

15. Controlling plants

It is useful to think of your pool as a well-fed version of a border. Plants introduced into ponds tend to grow quicker and better, owing to the abundance of water. In addition some species are aggressive and can easily dominate the ecosystem, so need regular control.

Planning a pond or pool

Ponds and pools differ in that a pond is a water-filled excavation, generally planted with marginal and aquatic plants, whereas a pool is a more architectural feature, more formalized and sometimes raised and contained above ground. The distinction has important implications on the successful design of your garden.

Making a new pond

The construction of a pond, with its water level at or just below ground level, involves substantial excavations, and disposal of the dug-up soil and subsoil can cause a major problem in a small garden. You may not be able to find a place in the garden to spread it so it may have to be removed. Bear in mind that excavated soil expands in volume by up to a third as it is dug up.

Ensure any level changes within the excavation are smoothly contoured and that the form is organic so that there are no tension points where a liner might tear as the water is introduced.

You also need to excavate an overflow from the pond, to maintain the water level and prevent flooding. This can be linked to a soakaway.

Pond liners

Once the pond hole is the required shape and size, it should be lined with geotextile fabric (see p206) and flexible waterproof material such as butyl rubber, which is sold in sheet form.

Measure the length and breadth of the excavation, adding the sides to each measurement. It is important to allow an additional margin in the sizing of the liner to account for settlement and stretching as the pond is filled with water, so add an extra 50–100cm (20–36in) to these dimensions. The excess material is either buried below paving alongside the pond or tucked back into the ground.

In order to obscure the liner (and create the illusion of a natural pool) you can plant suitable species within and alongside the water or overhang paving at the edge of the pond.

The weight of water

Water is a heavy – 1 cu m (35 cu ft) weighs one tonne. The subsequent pressure exerted against the butyl liner as the new pool is filled is sufficient to cause settlement within the excavation and potential punctures in the liner from any rubble or sharp objects buried beneath. For extra

---

DIY DESIGN

Controlling algae

- Gentle water movement will help to aerate and control water temperature within the pool. Simple jets and submersible pumps can achieve this.
- In some reflective pools chemical treatment will be necessary to prevent algal growth. A minimum depth of 70cm (28in) is also recommended to allow lower levels to remain cool.
- Filtration can be achieved with reed or gravel beds (shown right) containing micro-organisms that convert nutrients into usable plant foods or remove nutrient from the water. They rely on water drawn through the system using a pump. Ceramic or infrared filters can also work with pumped water.

protection you can also lay a bed of soft sand under the geotextile fabric.

If you wish to pave the edge of a butyl-lined pond then you can place the geotextile fabric over the butyl rubber to protect it from the paving above. The fabric need be used only where paving construction is planned, not across the whole pond.

Fill the pond slowly so the liner can be adjusted as the water level rises.

Pool designs

A pool generally has concrete foundations and waterproofed, concrete-block walls. Waterproofing materials are often black, helping to make the water surface reflective. In most cases a water depth of 70cm (28in) is recommended in order to prevent the water overheating.

The pool walls lend themselves to more formal and sharply defined pool designs. Paving can be easily added to the edge of the pool, supported by the solid walls beneath. An overhang in the paving will disguise the junction between the water and the construction alongside. Overflow systems need careful consideration as they will be visible.

Planting

The more ornamental and decorative the pool the less likely it is to be planted. Formal pools may require filtration, chemical treatment and sterilization to keep the water clear and pure. In such cases the pH balance of the pool may also need to be addressed, to prevent the build-up of limescale over time.

Clear water in shallow pools, such as this pebbled-base one, must be pumped through a filtration system or needs to be chemically treated, to avoid algae.

Found objects can often provide
interesting or unusual focal points such
as this old steel tank. The rust colours
are repeated in the surrounding planting.

… reflections change as you move around a pool…

A sheet of water just a few millimetres deep can create the illusion of depth. The effect relies on keeping the pool base and walls dark and the water slow-moving.

Mirrorlike water

The most important factor when planning to use water as a reflecting surface is that the interior of the pool or water feature must be dark. The water surface then acts as a mirror. Light pool liners reflect the light within the pool, thereby reducing surface reflections. Conveniently all pools become reflective after dark, as no light can penetrate the water.

Pool depth

The depth of water in a pool does not affect its ability to cause reflections. Indeed water depths of 1cm (¹/₂in) or less covering black powder-coated steel or dark stone such as basalt can produce spectacular images.

The visible construction in such pools is minimized, and the resulting reflections are maximized. This is an

important consideration if you want a reflective pool, as is the fact that a pool uses much less water than a pond and can be more easily maintained. When water is at such a premium nowadays, a pool is therefore an especially suitable choice for a small garden.

◀ **Consider what is reflected** in the surface of the pool, and the position from which you want to view it. A slightly canopied reflection, made by gunnera leaves, adds to the magic here.

What is reflected?

In tandem with the pool design you must consider what is to be mirrored in it. The success of the reflecting surface relies on the surroundings to the pool and your viewpoint. The reflections will change as you move around the garden. Looking down into the pool from alongside you will see the sky, but when sitting several metres away from the pool you will notice images of nearby walls, planting or tree canopies in the water.

A simple diagram showing your eye height and location, the position of the pool and the objects or plants around the pool will reveal probable images.

DIY DESIGN

Water for reflections

- Water that acts like a mirror can breathe life and colour into the garden, but it does need careful planning.
- To achieve the best reflections, the interior surfaces of the pond or pool must be black or dark in colour. A still pool produces the highest-quality images, but it is most likely to attract algae unless filtered (see p150).
- In infinity or overflowing pools, the reflections are contained by a sharply defined edge of gently cascading water with no apparent retention – magical!
- Think of how light will fall on your pool and more importantly on its backdrop, as this will produce dramatic reflections. Illuminate planting or objects beyond the pool to achieve this effect after dark.

Dynamic water

The mood of a garden can change dramatically with the sound and movement embodied in a fountain or cascade. These features can be incorporated into a pond or pool. Bear in mind that water disturbance is resented by some water plants such as waterlilies (*Nymphaea*). It also reduces reflective clarity.

A pump is required for any feature in which water flows, and it must be designed into the system together with the power source.

Fountains

The gentle sounds of water splashing from a fountain can helpfully disguise city or road noise pollution.

In a small gardens it is best to keep water jets low to prevent wind blow. Higher jets will be caught by wind eddies scattering water onto nearby surfaces and out of the system.

Water jets can be set into the ground at or just below the finished level of the paving, so the water splashes across the surface. This can reveal the coloration of the stone or produce interesting reflections. The water must be returned into the holding tank below the surface.

Narrow slot drains can be sited to catch the water runoff, or else gravel or other loose materials such as cobbles can be used to cover conduits or tanks below the surface, which will collect the water.

Cascades

A cascade is used to drop water into a receiving pool. Decorative spouts and letterbox systems can look effective in a small garden, where there is little space for a stream or rocky waterfall.

Traditionally a mask or face is mounted on a wall, where it can spout water into a receiving pool or basin. Ideally a screen wall behind the pool

▲ **The pipework for a wall spout** is often on the rear face. On a boundary wall, it would be inaccessible and an eyesore for a neighbour.

invisibly accommodates the pipework, which is attached to the rear face of the wall. Such a fixing is not suitable on a boundary wall, because of access problems for maintenance. On some surfaces it may be possible to recess the pipework into the wall or introduce plants to disguise the route.

Letterbox systems spread the cascade wide and deliver a gushing flow of water and a luxuriant sound. This avoids the noisier dripping sound of smaller spouts, which can be annoying. It is worth experimenting with the flow before making a decision.

Rills

A rill, which is a narrow, elongated cascade, can work well in a small garden, perhaps defining the central axis of a formal style. It must be clearly defined for safety and can be raised to provide interest along the edge of a planting bed.

◀ **Water can entertain and fascinate** even on a tiny scale. Here a simple pumped system based on a Japanese theme introduces sound and movement into the garden.

... meandering rills circulate and refresh the water...

This terrace and plunge pool are linked by meandering rills that recirculate the water after filtration, gently spilling and trickling into the enticing pool.

Planted water

Many water or moisture-loving plants offer dramatic and often larger-than-life foliage, and it may be this feature that you prefer above the enjoyment of open water.

The water's ecosystem

Plants work in different ways within water's ecosystem. Many submerged plants provide much-needed oxygen to water and so help to keep the ecosystem balanced, but these plants are not very visible from the surface.

Other species, known as emergents, grow primarily below the surface, but their flowering and leafy parts rise up into the air. Many of these species are also oxygenators. Waterlilies (*Nymphaea*) would fit into this category.

▲ *Gunnera manicata* will overwhelm a small pond as it makes its dramatic statement.

▲ **Marsh marigolds** are ideal planted in a bog garden and in a small planted pond.

How plants affect ponds

It is difficult initially to achieve a successful balance between plant growth and the overall balance of the water body in which they live. This is because plants introduced into a pond, or pool, draw their water needs from that pond, and this affects overall water levels. As the plant mass expands – enriched by nutrients in the water and a ready source of moisture –

DIY DESIGN

Bog gardens

- These can give new life to old ponds and introduce a wider diversity of planting into the garden.
- Drain and then perforate the base and sides of an existing pond. Make some small holes in a fibreglass or concrete-lined pond, to allow water seepage.
- To create a new bog garden requires the introduction of artificially impeded drainage. Lay butyl liner and then perforate it. Backfill with a shallow base layer of gravel, for drainage, covered by ordinary garden soil. Add plenty of well-rotted organic material to the soil before and after planting up the bog garden.
- Remember to water the bog garden from time to time.

▷ **Grasses and other 'transparent' plants** work well with water, catching light and often sparkling with dew or rain.

the burst in growth can sometimes be quite dramatic.

Therefore invasive plants and more aggressive reeds such as the narrow-leaved reedmace (*Typha latifolia*), should be avoided when making your plant selections, as their overvigorous nature will swamp your pond completely. The huge leaves of *Gunnera manicata* are a magnificent sight, frequently reaching 1.5m (5ft) in width, but again their sheer size makes them too dominant in a small garden even as a focal point.

Marginals and bog plants

Marginal plants like to have their feet in water but their main stems, foliage and flowers are borne above the water. Some irises are typical marginals.

Bog species enjoy damp or moisture-retentive ground. These habitats can be associated with ponds, although you can create a separate bog garden. Marsh marigolds (*Caltha palustris*) and hostas are typical bog plants, which enjoy these conditions.

Planting areas in the pond

It is important to design planting niches into the pond for the different types of plants. Many marginals like a water depth of 10–15cm (4–6in), but will spread into drier areas or deeper water. Shallow sloping banks will encourage this spread, and as foliage dies back the plants will often grow out over the detritus. These shallow banks also work well for wildlife colonization, but they need regular maintenance and control.

Alternatively, incorporate specific planting shelves with vertical walls or steep slopes into the deeper water to control these spreading tendencies.

Clearance of dead foliage within ponds remains an important part of maintaining the ecosystem. Without this maintenance work, ponds will become choked with debris.

Water swales and rills

Planting can also be undertaken in water catchment areas. The use of swales to absorb roof water or paving drainage for example will allow water to slowly seep back into the ground. The damp conditions that result are ideal for moisture-loving perennials.

Rills or shallow depressions can channel the water, and permeable materials such as gravel and cobbles can be used as surface mulches that stabilize the water surfaces. The water source will vary however, depending on weather conditions, so plants growing there need to be tolerant of both wet and dry conditions.

Achieving a natural balance in any pond or water feature takes time, especially when plants and wildlife are involved (as they invariably are).

Keeping water clear

Filtration is needed in most pools to keep the water clean and fresh.

Using pumps

Pumped systems require filters to prevent blockages, and even simple submersible pumps need to be protected. By lifting a pump off the base of a pond onto a low plinth much of the silt and sediment will drop below the main intake. Always check filters regularly to ensure water moves freely through the system.

Ceramic filters may be needed to trap some algae. Often UV light is also required to kill algae before removal.

Using plants

Reeds can be planted to clean 'grey' water from household waste. They can also be utilized in the filtration of natural swimming ponds. Most filtration beds use a system of planting into gravel, but the introduction of filtering bacteria within the gravel can allow the planting to be more

decorative, as it no longer contributes to the filtration process.

Nutrient-rich water

After filling a pool, the water often becomes green and opaque with algae. However, once the nutrient level in the water is exhausted, the water should start to clear.

If this does not occur, the pool may still be receiving nutrients from topped-up fresh water or from falling leaves and decaying plants.

What about fish?

If you introduce fish to your pond there is a greater risk of imbalance in the ecosystem, because of the introduction of extra waste. Ammonia will gradually build up, which is itself toxic to the fish. Nitrosomonas bacteria convert the ammonia to nitrite (also toxic), and nitrobacter then converts nitrites to beneficial nitrates, which is a plant and algae food.

You should therefore fit filter pads impregnated with appropriate bacteria into the water to keep the fish healthy and the water balanced. Extra pressure can occur on the filter and pump when the fish disturb the silt and sediment at the base of the pool.

Wildlife ponds

Fish view tadpoles and newts as a food source, and this can affect the balance of a wildlife pond's biodiversity.

▶ **Fish are fascinating**, alive with colour and movement, but they do increase the level of maintenance required in the garden.

Safety comes first with children and water

Water is an ever-present safety hazard within a garden, but the degree of risk has to be balanced by the enjoyment of the water itself. Young children are a major concern, as they will often underestimate the danger of deep water, which they will long to investigate. Their curiosity often gains the upper hand. Supervision and careful monitoring of children is by far the best option, as this approach can teach the benefits of water as a habitat and as a decorative element, while allowing the risks to be identified and underlined.

However it is still advisable to cover a pond or pool with a grille. Most will have to be custom-made in order to fit the specific shape of your water feature. By placing the cover just below the water surface its appearance will be less obvious, and the pool remains safe.

Raised pools may also have some deterrent element built in, so it becomes more difficult for a child to access the water. Underground storage of water for pools reduces or removes many of the dangers.

WATER:
CASE STUDY

WILD ABOUT WATER

In developing and modernizing the house at basement and ground floor level, Deborah Nagan has expanded her thinking into the garden, creating a generous light well that doubles as a relaxing oasis with tumbling water and leafy textures.

This is a garden of two characters. At the higher level the organic slate paving wanders through blazing dahlias and twining bean rows in an area designed to be viewed from ground level. The space is filled with luxuriant foliage and floral interest.

Basement area

The descent to basement level opens up a different world, separate from the surrounding city life. Because it is focused on the water, the space is full of movement from the pool and the cascade that drops the full height of the space. A simple, steel U-beam projects the water out over the pool, making a satisfying and lively focus. Plants reaching up to the higher level increase the sense of seclusion.

The pool interior is dark, suggesting great depth – like a jungle plunge pool – and the dark red of the garden wall adds to this rich and deceptive character. The moving water, filtered through recirculation, keeps the pool water fresh and clear.

Poolside planting

Planting down to the pool level is simple and minimal, with the filigree fronds of a soft tree fern spreading wide and low across the space. The shaded planting bed underneath is textured with cobblestones and planted with ferns. Vines tumble down from their sunnier planting positions in the higher garden, decorating the contrasting walls with their large, heart-shaped leaves.

Design ideas to take home

- Good exploitation of level change to add drama and activity to a tight space.
- Strong connections are made between house and garden.
- Use of strong colour and surface finishes establishes eye-catching contrasts.
- Bold foliage planting softens the architecture and dramatizes the setting with its waterfall.
- Changes in character are delivered by the different levels in the garden and by the choice of materials.

▲ **Rusting steel bars** in the border complement the dark red dahlias in early autumn. The bars are 1cm (½in) wide and can be bent by hand to form a dynamic curve that lasts all year round.

▶ **A shallow steel rill**, with rust adding to the texture, ingeniously carries water across the length of this tiny urban garden and then back to a waterfall.

... the forceful water drowns out unwanted noise from the city...

3

4

5

CITY PLUNGE

A narrow, steel rill (1) from the garden above projects water into the pool, with a dramatic splash. The sound of tumbling water penetrating this city garden light well drowns out unwanted noise from the city beyond.

Vines (*Vitis coignetiae*) (2) tumble down alongside to introduce vital, luxuriant foliage into the shady dell, visually breaking up the smooth rendered walls.

Timber steps (3) are disguised by the wide-spreading fronds of a soft tree fern (*Dicksonia antarctica*) (4). Its filigree leaves visually link the smaller ferns (5) with the planting above.

◀ **The depths of the light well** remain invisible from the main garden, where the reflections in the glazed wall are the only hint of the hidden surprise below.

SMALL GARDEN

PLANTING

For most people with a small garden, it is the plants that are most important, possibly because they are organic and constantly changing. Some gardeners prefer abundant flowers and foliage, while others adopt a more restrained attitude to planting.

For those inheriting a garden, design decisions can be complicated by the former owners' planting and different needs. However you should be bold and unsentimental in taking key decisions and in remoulding the garden to your requirements.

A challenge of a different sort occurs when you are the first person to move into a new-build property. Creating a garden from scratch requires clear foresight and purpose in order to imbue each space with a function as well as a welcoming atmosphere.

15 ways to... improve your planting design

1. Decide on the theme

Aim for an overall idea for your planting design instead of trying to fit in too many options, which can create confusion. A clear plan will help you to organize your plants too. Relate the idea to a style that links the garden with the interior of your house.

2. Work with the site

Understand the prevailing conditions in your garden before selecting plants. What is its orientation, and what are the patterns of light and shade during the course of a day? What soil do you have, and what is its moisture content? Although soil can be improved it is always better to choose the right plants for the right place.

3. Compile planting profiles

Produce written profiles of what you want the planting to do and then pick species to fit. The profile might include season of interest, height, texture, colour and perfume. Think about how you want plant associations to work rather than concentrating on plants as a collection of individuals.

4. Choose structural plants

Most planting schemes rely on structural or key plants, with their dominant characteristics such as form, foliage colour or branching structure. If these 'attitude' plants can be selected first, then it will be easier to consider how the supporting or associated plants might work.

5. Plan crops

Even a small garden provides a great opportunity to supplement your diet with edible produce, but the emphasis must be on supplement. Plan the garden so you get maximum cropping from each area. However you do need to be realistic about how much food you can grow to feed a small family – or even just yourself.

6. Plant for scale

Fewer larger-scale plants in a small garden generate visual interest and should relate successfully to the surrounding architecture or garden features. Numerous small plants on the other hand can make a small garden look overcrowded. With their greater variety and number, they will also need more care and attention.

7. Plant for privacy

Lack of privacy is one of the main sources of irritation in a small garden, especially in an urban centre in which the surrounding buildings can be disproportionately tall. Climbers, hedges and trees can be planted so their higher canopies or screens offer some protection. The disadvantage of using plants in this way is that they increase the shade within the garden.

8. Plant for coherence

A single species looks good when repeated several times within a planting scheme, and it can be used in larger groups too. Both techniques will simplify plant selection and the overall impression of the garden, and contribute to a sense of rhythm and coherence.

9. Plant for vertical interest

Tall plants are invaluable in small garden spaces, in which the vertical scale is often limitless. The careful selection of compact, taller species, that is without a wide-spreading form, will introduce a dynamic quality to the planting. Study the three-dimensional form of the plants you shortlist.

10. Consider plant density

You need to achieve a balance between the predicted spread of a plant and soil that looks bare because too much space has been left between plants. Open soil is prone to weed infestation, and part of the reason for planting is to reduce that eventuality. Conversely, if planting is too dense, the form and decorative impact of specific plants can be lost. Plan for 3–5 years ahead, but remember that most textbooks provide mature spread data.

11. Plant for diversity

Group plants together according to the insects that they might attract as a group or association, rather than plant them as individuals. Also consider the plants in neighbourhood gardens and how you can contribute to a wider range of biodiversity, to the benefit of your locality.

12. Select colour

When designing with colour initially you should take into account the context of the whole garden, so consider backdrops and paving colours as well as the plants themselves. The most lively colour combinations are provided by flowers, yet these are often short-lived, whereas foliage colour is more long-lasting.

13. Plant in containers

Select the largest containers possible, so that the maximum amount of moisture can be captured and stored in the growing medium. Use asssociated plants within one container, rather than disparate ones. Meanwhile, a mass planting of a single variety or a specimen plant can be allowed its own container so that the true glory can be appreciated.

14. Establish associations

Part of the joy of planting design is the relationship you create between totally unrelated species. Look for characteristics that plants have in common – leaf shape, flower colour, form – and relate plants accordingly. Some contrast is useful too.

15. Be honest

Well-designed planting relies for its success on how well the plants are looked after. Consequently it is an essential part of planting design to be honest about how much maintenance work will be required, and how often it needs doing. Your appropriate level of time, interest and expertise can then be factored into the design.

Planting habitats

Plants can be divided loosely according to their natural habitats in the landscape. By thinking of plants in this way, optimum decisions can be made on plant selection. Water planting, wetland communities, field and meadow, woodland edge and woodland each combine plants that share similarities or grow together well as communities.

Wetland

Wetland planting can be appropriate for damp or poorly drained soils or can be artificially created. It includes many large-leaved and bold foliage plants such as plantain lily (*Hosta*) and rodgersia as well as many reeds with tall and elegant foliage. Colour can also be a rich source of interest, as many irises, primroses (*Primula*), ligularias and even some bergamots (*Monarda*) enjoy damp conditions. Wetland plants require a combination of sun and moisture, so shade limits the plant options.

Top 5 wetland plants

Butomus umbellatus – for water edges and margins; large, pink flowerheads in summer
Caltha palustris – prefers bog or marginal conditions; bright yellow flowers in spring
Lythrum virgatum 'Dropmore Purple' – for damp pool edges or margins; purple flower spikes
Persicaria bistorta 'Superba' – good as ground cover in moist soils; pink, bottlebrush flowers.
Schoenoplectus lacustris subsp. *tabernaemontani* (syn. *Scirpus lucustris* subsp. *tabernaemontani*) – elegant and tall marginal; fine grasslike foliage

Also try hosta, primula, rodgersia, thalictrum and zantedeschia

Keep existing conditions

With climate change and sustainability increasingly affecting garden-making, it is particularly important to work with existing wetland conditions. Soil improvement and drainage with the aim of altering soil conditions to grow a wider range of plants are rarely successful in the long term.

Wetland in action

Reed beds to filter grey water can be enhanced decoratively by introducing varied wetland plants. Swales to take excess surface drainage or roof water can be similarly planted up. Puncture an artificial liner that is normally used to retain water for a pond and lay it below ground to slow the rate of drainage and so establish artificial bog or wetland conditions.

Bulrush (*Typha*) is generally invasive and needs to be carefully managed in water filtration beds. Use *T. minima* in bog gardens.

Native meadows are home to grasses, perennials and annuals. Their beauty can be enhanced by ornamental alternatives.

Field & meadow

These habitats provide one of the richest sources of garden planting, because they contain many perennials (often known as herbaceous perennials), grasses and bulbs. Although some perennials and grasses grow quite tall, the main characteristic of this habitat is that it harbours lower-growing and comparatively well-behaved species.

A wide variety of plants flourish in fields and meadows. Some of these species rarely grow out of control. This is good news for small garden owners who might want to use these meadows plants. Certain of these species also grow in woodlands, so it is feasible to find perennials for any shaded meadow area in a small garden.

Perennials and grasses

Once established, a perennial poppy (*Papaver orientale*) or ornamental grass grows to the same height each year and dies back in winter. Some such as plantain lilies disappear altogether, while many grasses or perennials such as coneflowers (*Rudbeckia*) retain their seedheads and old foliage until the end of winter. You should then cut back the plants, so new growth can take over.

Bulbs in meadows

Rather than planting an area with just one species, include some bulbs between the plants. Early-season ones can add an extra dimension to field and meadow planting schemes, especially when interplanted. Such bulbs will either extend the season of interest or add depth and colour to the basic planting scheme.

Prairies and ornamental meadows

Traditionally these perennials and grasses often used to spread as they mature and so needed regular division or splitting to keep them under control. Fortunately this is no longer the case, because of the introduction of clump-forming or less vigorous varieties and limited self-seeding plants. The resulting communities are often referred to as prairies or ornamental meadows.

Their dynamic growth cycles, predictable growth rates, often excellent flower colouring and highly transparent foliage in the grasses means that prairie and ornamental meadow plants are highly appropriate in small garden design.

Top 10 perennials & grasses

Achillea 'Walther Funcke' – Orange-red, flat flowerheads contrast well with grasses
Calamagrostis x *acutiflora* 'Karl Foerster' – tall and vertical grass clumps; looks good into winter
Deschampsia cespitosa 'Goldtau' – soft, airy, shade-tolerant grasses
Macleaya cordata – tall; grey felted leaves; buff flowerheads
Miscanthus sinensis 'Ferner Osten' – midheight grass; early to flower; red panicles
Molinia caerulea subsp. *caerulea* 'Heidebraut' – delicate, transparent flowerheads look good well into winter
Panicum virgatum 'Heavy Metal' – prairie grass; grey-green foliage
Phlomis russeliana – drought tolerant; felted leaves; lemon flowers; good winter seedheads
Rudbeckia fulgida var. *sullivantii* 'Goldsturm' – bold yellow daisies
Salvia nemorosa 'Caradonna' – deep purple-blue flower spikes

◄ **The flowers of *Ammi majus* create a filigree** of lace through which the deep blue flowers of salvia and ferny green cosmos emerge.

Top 10 annuals & biennials

Ammi majus – tall; fine, light foliage; lacy, white, flat flowerheads that float in the air

Cosmos bipinnatus – saucer flowers carried over ferny foliage; many cultivars such as carmine 'Dazzler' and white 'Purity'

Digitalis ferruginea – tall spikes of rusty brown/apricot flowers; interplant with grasses

***Echium vulgare* 'Blue Bedder'** – dense, blue flower spikes borne over dark green basal foliage; a magnet for bees

Nicotiana sylvestris – tall and stately; long, white, trumpet-shaped flowers with rich evening scent

Nigella damascena 'Miss Jekyll' – cottage-garden favourite with a froth of feathery foliage surrounding delicate sky blue flowers

Onopordum acanthium – tall, silvery white thistles; suitable for sunny gravel plantings; popular with insects and birds

Papaver somniferum – wide range of colour and flower types in the red-purple spectrum; decorative, grey-green foliage

***Salvia viridis* 'Blue'** – one of many annual salvias that bear deep blue flowers throughout summer

Verbascum olympicum – tall; felted leaves and stems; sulphur-yellow flowers; good for gravel planting

Annuals

Annual species (those completing their life cycles within one year) are also typical field or meadow plants. Generally they rely on their strong flower colour and dense planting for effect.

Traditionally, annuals were associated with civic pride, summer bedding displays or added to more permanent garden planting, especially in Victorian or Edwardian gardens.

Annuals with longer impact

The growth of the pictorial meadow in the 21st century, spurred on by researchers such as Nigel Dunnett at Sheffield University, in the UK, has transformed ideas about annuals.

Annuals are now planted so they create impact and waves of colour throughout the main growing season. Although designed for larger spaces, successional annual planting has clear advantages for a small garden, where colour and interest can be introduced for little more than the price of a few packets of seeds.

The planting needs to be cleared each year, so that new annuals can be sown. Alternatively the sowing of secondary, winter crops or quick-maturing vegetables can provide a decorative and useful filler.

Designer Brita von Schoenaich used this technique in the planting of the rectangular borders outside the Tate Britain art gallery in London.

Hedgerows

The hedgerow has been a common feature of the landscape for centuries, used as a form of enclosure or as boundaries to land ownership in many countries. Frequently the species used would be remnants from older woodlands or from the edges of woodland, where shrubs and trees grow together. Once mature, hedges provide good nesting habitats and feeding stations for wildlife.

Many species can be used for hedging, from grasses to trees, and it is normally the trimming or the regimentation of the linear planting that provides the hedge form.

Popular hedges

Evergreen yew (*Taxus baccata*) is a favourite garden hedge, becoming dense and dark as regular trimming develops a finely branching network. Alternatively deciduous species such as hornbeam (*Carpinus betulus*) and beech (*Fagus sylvatica*) work well in a small garden, because they retain their coppery autumnal foliage over winter and so bring interest to the garden for most of the year.

Pleached hedges

In a form known as pleaching, the foliage is maintained on top of clear tree trunks, creating a screen at high level under which you can walk or add additional planting. This particular form of hedge planting is useful to provide privacy or visual screening from unwanted views. Good deciduous species for such treatment are lime (*Tilia*) and hornbeam. Try holm oak (*Quercus ilex*) for evergreen pleaching.

Columns and spheres

Single columns or blocks of hedge can establish a successful sense of order in what can sometimes be unruly perennial-dominated planting. Box (*Buxus sempervirens*) is often planted in this way as an edge to a border or planting area. It can be pruned into low, rectangular cushions or spheres, which are ideal shapes for smaller spaces. Box is evergreen, so it retains its obvious structure over winter.

▼ **The finely ribbed leaves** of hornbeam provide bright green cover in summer and are retained throughout winter in their coppery, autumnal tones.

Top 5 hedging plants

Buxus sempervirens – evergreen; tiny, glossy, midgreen leaves; ideal for low hedges and parterres; several forms available
Carpinus betulus – deciduous; veined, midgreen leaves; retains coppery autumnal foliage into winter
Fagus sylvatica – deciduous; glossy, wavy-edged leaves retained in coppery tones into winter; coloured foliage forms
Prunus lusitanica – evergreen; larger, glossy-leaved alternative to *Taxus baccata*
Taxus baccata – evergreen; traditional English garden plant; dense, dark green block of foliage makes good backdrop to planting

Note that hedging species will typically grow into trees unless regularly pruned into shape

Shrubs

Shrubs, identifiable by their multiple woody stems, come in a wide range of species, varying in height from less than 1m (3ft) up to 8–10m (25–30ft) and often eventually spreading to a similar extent. They are found in scrubby areas and woodland edges, where they might mix with perennials and grasses, or grow as low-level plants in woodland. Some shrubs as a result are tolerant of shade.

Selection criteria

Given their variations in height and spread it is important to match shrubby species to the space you have available. Careful pruning can curtail plant growth, but this may need to be carried out at specific times to ensure that flowering is not affected.

Apart from size, plant selection can be determined by bark and branch colour, foliage texture and colour, flower colour and perfume, and fruit and autumn coloration if the shrub is deciduous. Some shrubs such as witch hazel (*Hamamelis*) or daphnes produce their strongly scented flowers during winter.

The form of the shrub is important too, as some with central stems allow planting below the canopy.

▼ **Rosehips extend the** period of interest from autumn into winter, well beyond the original summer flowers. Shrub roses tend to produce the best hips.

Top 10 shrubs

Cornus alba 'Sibirica' – scarlet winter stems; flat, cream flowerheads; good autumn colour; other cultivars available

Cotinus coggygria – soft, feathery seed clusters; grown mainly for its autumn colour

Euphorbia mellifera – narrow, elegant foliage; domed form; fragrant flowers in spring

Exochorda x *macrantha* 'The Bride' – spring interest; rounded, fresh green leaves; prolific display of white flowers

Hamamelis mollis – deciduous; scented flowers in winter

Philadelphus 'Belle Etoile' – deciduous; deliciously fragrant, white flowers in summer; reasonably compact

Rosa – a huge range of options available but try *R*. Munstead Wood for strong colour and scent; *R*. Burgundy Ice for deep velvet floral tones; *R*. 'Geranium' for colourful hips

Sambucus nigra f. *porphyrophylla* 'Eva' – deciduous; dark purple/ black, dissected foliage; pink flowers; cut back each winter for autumn colour

Sarcococca confusa – evergreen; tiny, white, richly scented flowers in winter

Viburnum tinus 'Eve Price' – evergreen; good for screening views; small, dark green leaves; pink-white flowers and metallic-blue berries in winter

◄ **The scented winter flowers** of *Hamamelis* x *intermedia* 'Jelena' are a colourful spectacle in late winter. These shrubs are most successful when planted in groups and in light shade.

The delicate flowers of juneberry appear fleetingly in early summer. They are followed by soft green foliage that colours well during autumn.

Woodland edge & woodland

These two habitats are the domain of trees, with woodland edge typically formed of smaller tree species and larger shrubs, while woodland itself is dominated by larger trees.

Woodland trees

The larger tree species such as lime (*Tilia*), beech (*Fagus*) and holm oak (*Quercus ilex*) are often useful in a smaller garden in hedge form, while table-pruned plane (*Platanus*) trees and some maples (*Acer*) successfully combine delicate tracery with larger, textured leaves.

Canopies and habit

It is helpful to look at factors such as vertical interest and sense of scale when assessing a tree's suitability for a small garden. The transparency of the foliage canopy and the branching habit are also important. Trees such as birch (*Betula*), sorbus or sophora will generate light shade, without growing out of control, and multistemmed specimens will often be lower in height than single-trunk ones.

When densely planted, trees such as birch grow taller and thinner, with a more limited canopy, as they reach up, competing for the light. Smaller but characterful trees include sumach (*Rhus*), juneberry (*Amelanchier*), smaller maples and magnolia.

Combined planting

It is possible to mix plants, as in their original habitats. Woodlands for example often include trees, shrubs, perennials and grasses. When selecting your combination consider shade and light levels carefully, and bear in mind inherent competition from the surrounding planting.

The shade from a tree in a small garden cannot be ignored and, unless the tree dies or is removed, there is little that will change the prevailing shade conditions or the relative dryness of the soil below. Therefore, in designing for this situation, you should start with the conditions as a limiting factor and then compile your planting palette appropriately.

A selective approach

Rather than choosing species from each planting type, simplify and restrict your selection. For example, species of the meadow category can form a relatively uniform planting layer into which you plant specimen trees to produce a sense of space. Multi-stemmed tree specimens will increase visual interest. Or use clipped hedge species as columns or short blocks to contrast with looser perennials.

Planting styles

The way colour, plants, materials and space are utilized in a garden reflects its style and inherent patterns. These tend to be overlaid onto gardens to symbolize a particular approach or to produce a coherent scheme. A stylistic approach can be true to its reference, or you can mix or fuse references to make your own combinations.

Formal-garden planting

Although often classified as a style in its own right (see p66), formal planting appears in a wide range of design styles from classical to Arts and Crafts (see p74). Its key component is symmetry. Areas of geometric lawn are typical, with planting ordered into rows or repeated on each side of an axis.

The repeated planting of shrubs or specimen plants in an avenue or half-avenue format can work well. Alternatively consider using clipped climbers along boundary walls in the same repeated pattern.

Hedges are also used as repeated features within a garden, as well as to define border edges. Associated planting is often simple ground cover, echoing the classical gardens of Italy and France. Gardens influenced by the English flower garden style (see p178) include balanced hedging, but the border planting is more varied and is inspired by the Arts and Crafts period.

▼ **Hedges are key features** in formal garden design. Symmetrical borders may be richly planted or filled in a much simpler style.

Cottage-garden planting

This style is often seen as a peculiarly British one. It comprises highly varied and seemingly abundant plants, which burst out of every patch of available space in the garden. This produces an *ad hoc* charm that is undeniably beguiling, especially in summer when most of the species typical of cottage-garden planting will be flowering.

These however are fairly high-maintenance gardens, which need time and energy spent in pruning, splitting and weeding in order to keep the system balanced.

Dense planting

In cottage-garden planting, many planting types are mixed together, often in an apparently random way. Trees such as yew (*Taxus baccata*), holly (*Ilex*) or hornbeam (*Carpinus*) are often pruned into topiary shapes or hedges to create separate areas. Between these grow a mix of some shrubs and a higher proportion of densely planted perennials, which are often allowed to spill over onto paths.

Roses are typical of cottage gardens, as are scented flowers such as phlox. Self-seeders such as valerian (*Centranthus*) and lady's mantle (*Alchemilla mollis*) are allowed to proliferate throughout the garden.

Other features

Small areas of lawn or hard paving exist alongside deep borders. Many cottage gardens also include fruit and vegetables (see also p77).

◀ **Cottage-garden planting** is often dominated by summer-flowering perennials, to which annuals may be added. The effect is glorious but high in maintenance.

Clipped but asymmetrically placed features are a key to the Modernist garden, where the contrast between vertical and horizontal features is emphasized as much as possible.

Modernist planting

There is a strong relationship with Japanese design here, especially in the planting design (see p179).

Contrast and harmony

A key characteristic is the contrast between vertical and horizontal elements. Plants or blocks of planting that emphasize this difference should harmonize well with any architecture that shares these qualities. The result should be an elegant, controlled and spacious exploration of planting, for which a limited palette of species is selected for specific purposes.

Hedges partially define spaces within the garden, where planting is often organized in rectangular blocks using a single species of shrub or perennial within each block for colour or texture. Shrubs or trees are incorporated as sculptural specimens selected for their specific character. They may be planted singly or repeated in a line of three (see also p68).

DIY DESIGN

Variations on a single colour

- Often gardeners mix colours to achieve impact, but by reducing the colour range your experience of colour can be greatly intensified and made more atmospheric.
- Select a key flower colour, perhaps red, and then look for tonal variations on that colour to use alongside it. A red-purple flower will enhance the sense of depth, whereas a red-orange hue will visually bring the flower closer. The overall effect will still be red. For more help in selecting associated colours, see p52–53.
- When purple is used alongside red it is seen as a warm colour. When purple is used with blue it will be seen as a cooler colour. The adoption of a limited planting palette simplifies the design process, yet adds drama.

Mediterranean planting

Although the Mediterranean as a region covers a vast range of habitats and garden types, the Mediterranean planting style generally refers to the dry gravel gardens that reflect the maquis terrain of southern France, Spain and Italy (see also pp80–81).

Gravel covers both paths and planting areas, so planting beds are generally not defined. Plants grow through the gravel, which acts as a weed suppressant. This enables planting to be open and informal, because the main task of outcompeting the weeds is already taken care of.

The planting is a mixture of low-growing perennials, shrubs and small trees, which are positioned in apparently random groups across the garden. Clipped hedges – of box (*Buxus*), for example – are frequently placed as accent plants or where they can define areas within the garden.

Edible or scented

Specimen trees such as bay laurel (*Laurus nobilis*), olive (if local climate allows), broom (*Genista*, *Cytisus*) or wattle (*Acacia*) can be selected for their gnarled or windswept appearance. Spurge (*Euphorbia*), lavender and rock rose (*Cistus*) are typical choices for lower shrubs or perennials.

Grasses such as feather grass (*Stipa*) have a softening effect and look good planted with ornamental onions (*Allium*) and creeping thyme. Much of the planting is scented, and many culinary herbs such as rosemary are typical of this habitat.

◀ **The strident contrast** between blue *Nepeta racemosa* 'Walker's Low' and orange *Diascia* Little Tango in this Monaco-inspired garden is supported by the sharp, sword-shaped leaves of *Yucca aloifolia* behind.

English flower-garden planting

Although this planting style developed from the Arts and Crafts movement of the early 20th century (see p74), it came to prominence as the quintessential English garden only in the later decades of that century, through garden designers such as Rosemary Verey and Penelope Hobhouse.

Successional colour

The approach is border based, and it generally borrows from the formal layouts and hedged compartments of gardens by Sir Edwin Lutyens and Gertrude Jekyll. Shrubs and perennials are planted in carefully colour-themed associations of flower and foliage, for successional colour from late spring through to autumn.

Each differently colour-themed planting display is then surrounded by a hedge of yew (*Taxus baccata*) or hornbeam (*Carpinus*). Boundary walls can be used as backdrops in this way.

In a small garden the number of colour themes should be reduced, because of the limited space.

A challenge in winter

Such high-maintenance planting schemes require careful balancing to ensure successional interest. Particular thought needs to be given to the winter period, when the perennial-dominated garden will be dormant. However if shrubs are planted for winter interest, then the planting scheme will lose its integrity as a summer flower garden.

▶ **The popularity of the Arts and Crafts style** is based on colour associations principally using perennials and biennials. Here the repetition of lady's mantle (*Alchemilla mollis*) holds the complex composition together.

Japanese planting

In a small Japanese-style garden, trees are restricted to small species or are pruned to a specific shape (see p79). The shrubs can be densely planted and clipped to form low but expansive, organic, hedgelike forms.

This careful management of trees and shrubs is often omitted from Western interpretations, with the result that much of the magic and character of these gardens are lost.

Typical plant choices

Japanese maples (*Acer japonicum*, *A. palmatum*), birch (*Betula*), bamboos, camellias or dwarf pines are popular choices for structural or key plants, while plantain lily (*Hosta*), sweet box (*Sarcococca*), rhododendron, or nandina are planted for their low-mound-forming habit.

Moss is also a favourite, frequently planted under trees with light canopies to contribute to an abstracted woodland landscape.

Paving textures are used here to give directional movement to the garden. Planting provides contrasting foliage and screening, while boulders offer a focal point.

Creating a layered habitat

- Plants tend to grow as loose types or communities, which can be manipulated in layers in a small garden.
- Typical planting layers in the landscape are low grasses and ground cover; meadow-level plants; shrubs and hedges; and woodland. Although all of these can be represented within a garden, a limited selection of layers can open up the structure and simplify planting.
- Multistemmed trees such as juneberry (*Amelanchier*), apple (*Malus*) or dogwood (*Cornus*) planted into an ornamental meadow layer will bring light and open space into the garden. Colour and textural interest is incorporated into the lower planting, and the trees can be strategically located to disguise or block views.

The majestic leaves of *Tetrapanax papyrifer* 'Rex' dominate this foliage composition with castor oil plant (*Ricinus communis*) and feathery palm *Phoenix canariensis*.

Naturalistic planting

Naturalistic planting has been popular in garden-making for centuries, albeit in different guises. The aim generally is to reflect nature in some form, not necessarily to copy it directly. A key influence in the late 19th century was William Robinson, who expounded the virtues of combining exotic and native plants in a single scheme.

In the 20th century, Robinson's original concepts were developed and refined in the Netherlands and Germany, while in Britain the style lapsed in favour of a more ornamental and decorative approach.

Continental Europe

What is now known as the New Perennial Movement uses a palette of grasses and perennials planted in large groups, or drifts, for broad sweeps of colour and texture. Strong flower colour from sage (*Salvia*), cranesbill (*Geranium*) or bergamot (*Monarda*) is often softened by transparent grasses such as purple moor grass (*Molinia*), feather grass (*Stipa*) and crab grass (*Panicum*).

Because much of the planting is dominated by perennials and grasses, clipped hedges are often introduced to provide a sense of order and structure.

British approach

With this ecological planting style, the plant is selected from the same habitat but not necessarily from the same country or continent (see also p82). This allows for diversity while reducing the chances of more aggressive species dominating.

By restricting the planting palette it is possible to design in this way for a small space. Perennials and grasses are often selected for their autumn and winter colour and seedheads.

Foliage planting

As Europeans travelled to ever more exotic places in the 19th century their appetite for plants that echoed those locations grew. Fortunately many of these exotic plants can thrive in the warmer urban centres of cool-temperate regions.

Profuse vegetation

The aim with foliage planting is to fill the garden with bold plant forms and oversized foliage, suggesting a jungle (see p84) or oasis. Planting should be in large blocks or beds within garden boundaries that are ambiguous. It should include eye-catching, tall grasses such as miscanthus mixed with bamboos, bananas (*Musa*) and phormium, with the emphasis on their dramatic leaf shapes and textures.

Flowers for drama

Any flowers need to match the drama of the foliage. The strong colours of dahlia, canna, montbretia (*Crocosmia*) and day lilies (*Hemerocallis*) work in this respect, producing splashes and sparks of colour.

Annuals can also be used in this way. Plant them on a seasonal basis, or grow them in pots, which can be easily moved into and out of position.

Prairie planting combines textured grasses, colourful perennials and bulbs in layered, sequential positions and apparently random mixes, often termed naturalistic in style.

Productive planting can be successfully integrated into an ornamental garden. These purple cabbages growing alongside tall lines of elegant sweet corn echo the colouring of the transparent spread of *Verbena bonariensis*.

Productive planting

Vegetable, fruit and herb gardening has enjoyed something of a renaissance in the early 21st century because of much greater interest in where food comes from. Family gardens therefore frequently include an area for food production.

To some extent the decision on where to grow your crops relies on how much time you have available and on the needs of the cropping plants (see p212). These need careful thought in the initial design process.

Traditionally vegetable, fruit and herbs were grown in a separate space or in an entire garden seen as distinct from the decorative borders and formal areas. The trend now is to give productive plants a more central role in garden design or to combine them with more decorative plants.

Mixed planting beds

Many herbs grow quite happily among other plants, and soft fruit such as raspberry or red- and blackcurrants will also share planting space. Other crops such as potatoes, carrots, lettuce and cabbage need dedicated space either in rows or in raised beds. More decorative plants can be used at the edge of vegetable

▲ **Dwarf apple trees** sit neatly alongside raised timber planting beds. The higher planters allow for easier access and care of crops such as these peppers.

beds, or be interplanted between the vegetable rows, in what is known as companion planting.

DIY DESIGN

Edible crops in a small space

- You need to be quite imaginative to grow fruit, vegetables and herbs successfully in a small garden, because only a very limited area is available.
- Use wall space and windowsills for hanging baskets and troughs filled with edible plants, or try out a vertical planting system (see p122).
- If you have sufficient sunshine, grow herbs such as chives, mint, rocket, sage or basil, which can be harvested regularly throughout summer.
- Cut-and-come again vegetables such as spinach and chard occupy little space and can be regularly harvested. The young leaves of celery, lettuce and peas are very tasty in salads.

Contrasts in foliage texture are pronounced in this composition of clipped box (*Buxus sempervirens*) spheres and fine-leaved *Hakonechloa macra*. Circular pools of reflective water create a sense of stillness.

Minimalist planting

Minimalism grew out of Modernism (see p68) and is a more extreme development of its loss of unnecessary decoration. It celebrates the purity of simple and essential elements. In planting design a Minimalist style thus lies at the opposite end of the design spectrum to the hugely varied cottage-garden style (see p175).

Utter simplicity

Minimalist planting design relies on the careful selection of the perfect plant for any given situation and on minimizing of the planting palette. At its most extreme this may entail using only a single species – or even a single plant – within a garden.

Although a tree is sometimes chosen for just one characteristic, a tree with a range of seasonal interest is more likely to be chosen. Juneberry (*Amelanchier*), catalpa, birch (*Betula*) or Japanese maples (*Acer japonicum*, *A. palmatum*) fall in this latter category, because they share many of the following attributes – spring interest, flowers, berries, bark interest, autumn colour or decorative form.

Broad blocks

A dense ground cover of grasses such as *Stipa tenuissima* interplanted with a range of bulbs such as ornamental onion (*Allium*) or quamash (*Camassia*) are a typical planting scheme with an extended period of interest. Simple, ordered blocks of climbers such as *Clematis armandii*, which produces vertical, glossy, evergreen foliage, or perfumed, evergreen star jasmine (*Trachelospermum jasminoides*) can be planted so they screen walls and maximize use of space.

Conceptualist planting

In Conceptualist planting design you select the plants and possibly also the method of planting so they express your ideas and concepts, by repeating blocks of texture perhaps or by including intense pools or masses of colour in a rich and diverse palette (see also p73).

Invaluable components

Perennials and annuals work well in this genre, because they provide concentrated colour, which is frequently invoked to express Conceptualist ideas. Strong blocks of foliage colour can reinforce these messages too.

Transparency or foliage texture and plant form can also be planted in this way, although planting is often dense or repeated in order to obtain specific effects and visual drama.

Sustainable planting

Sustainability has many different interpretations – recycling, renewable resources, biodiversity, conservation and organic gardening – but they all relate in some way to the concept and philosophy of the sustainable garden.

As a planting style, the intention with sustainability is to create a

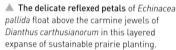

▲ **The delicate reflexed petals** of *Echinacea pallida* float above the carmine jewels of *Dianthus carthusianorum* in this layered expanse of sustainable prairie planting.

balanced community of species that thrives ecologically as a habitat (not necessarily decorative) but needs little or no imput once established. This involves assessing the conditions within the garden and planting to those conditions, rather than changing the soil, for example through the input of improvers or organic matter.

It is possible, however, to have an artificial area of wetland or marginal plants (see p158) fed in a sustainable conditions by using 'grey' water cleansed in a filtration bed (see p160).

Low-nutrient soils

Many ecosystems exist on poor soils and few nutrients, so you need to ignore the basic rule of gardening about regular feeding of the soil.

In many gardens soil nutrient levels actually need to be lowered to allow less competitive flowering plants to thrive. In fact James Hitchmough of Sheffield University, in the UK, has found that prairie seed mixes establish best on a bed of brick dust and sand.

▼ **Brilliant red stepping stones** or 'platelets' meander through damp meadow planting interspersed with the contrasting, blood red flowers of *Paeonia* 'Buckeye Belle'.

Planning for long- and short-term

For some people, their current property is a permanent residence for the foreseeable future, while for others it is a short-term staging post. Planting schemes need to reflect these respective situations.

Short-term viewpoint

In a garden planned for short-term use it is probably best to plant edible crops or else annuals, perennials, grasses, climbers and small shrubs. These reach maturity relatively quickly and are also comparatively low in cost. Perennials and grasses in particular can be purchased in small pots, and they will then grow rapidly to create a dense and convincing impact. Larger shrubs and trees take longer to establish, so avoid these as you may be passing on planting challenges to future occupants of your property.

Long-term perspective

For those intending to occupy a property for the longer term, why not invest in a larger plant such as a tree, so you can enjoy watching it develop into a fully mature specimen.

A young tree is relatively cheap to buy and should establish and grow quickly, but there will still be a period of several years before it makes any real impact in the garden.

More mature trees and larger shrubs are available, but they do cost considerably more, depending on their overall size, character and rarity. They may also be more difficult to establish. For long-term residents these higher costs may seem worthwhile.

Adapting the scheme

Changing soil conditions such as those under a recently planted tree need to be taken into account in the long-term garden plan. As the tree canopy increases and the garden becomes more shady, the original planting under the canopy will struggle and may need replacing by shade-lovers.

DIY DESIGN

Layered bulbs in containers

- Bulbs will always bring welcome colour into the garden, but in small spaces their impact can be lost among other plants.
- Plant each bulb two to three times its height deep.
- By planting into containers you can emphasize the seasonal impact of bulbs, especially by combining a range of species. Layer the bulbs as you fill the pot. Large bulbs such as daffodils (*Narcissus*) require deeper planting than smaller ones such as snowdrops (*Galanthus*) and crocuses, which start the season.
- Plant for a gradual succession of interests or for a bold display of combined colours.

Informal groups of foxgloves (*Digitalis*), woodrush (*Luzula*) and ostrich fern (*Matteuccia struthiopteris*) nestle in the shade of light-canopied *Zelkovia serrata* 'Green Vase' and the open foliage of bottlebrush buckeye (*Aesculus parviflora*).

Putting plants together

Planting beds or areas should be as large as possible even in a small garden. This maximizes rainfall catchment and increases the impact of planting (see p45). It allows larger-scale plants to be used, helping to establish good depth, height, scale and proportion in the design.

Plant height and spread

Plants are often described in books and nursery catalogues by their height and spread. It is helpful to know what the mature height of the plant is likely to be, as such information is broadly accurate. Spread measurements are much more variable, because it is often based on optimum conditions, and it ignores the impact of surroundings and competing plants.

Individual plants perform very differently when planted alongside other plants, and their planting spreads vary accordingly, even though anticipated heights generally remain as described. In some cases, especially with young trees, dense planting will curtail spread dimensions but will increase height, as each plant competes for light.

Plants on plans

In diagrammatic form, plants are often represented as circles. Therefore a plant with a spread of 60cm (24in) is shown as a circle with a 60cm (24in) diameter. By placing a series of circles together with their circumferences just touching, you can calculate what is known as the planting centres and also how many plants will be required in a given area. This is often shown

as plants per sq m (sq yd). It may be possible to plant three 60cm (24in) spread plants into a sq m (sq yd). The eventual, mature shapes of plants set at such a spacing would look like a series of cushionlike mounds.

However a young, mound-forming plant such as a santolina would take some time to reach its 60cm (24in) spread. In the meantime there would be open soil, in which weeds might seed and so lead to increased upkeep.

Overlapping plants

Instead, if you overlap each 60cm (24in) circle by 10cm (4in) on the planting plan, each plant then occupies only 50cm (20in). The plants grow together more quickly, and their shape is more of a rippling or undulating block than a mound.

Using this overlapping method, the number of santolina plants per sq m (sq yd) will increase from three to four. Therefore this method of planting is more expensive but it has reduced weed invasion because the soil is covered more effectively.

Greater density

Finally, you can increase planting density further by overlapping the circles by 20cm (8in). Each plant then occupies only 40cm (16in), and the density increases to six plants per sq m (sq yd). The plants grow together rapidly, forming a more consistent mass of plants and losing some of the mounding characteristic of the santolina. This is the most expensive form of planting, but it reduces maintenance in the short

▲ **Santolina is used here** as a continuous edging plant to define a formal herb bed. It has been planted unusually close to achieve this effect.

term because the soil between the plants is covered quickly. In the longer term, it may be necessary to reduce overcrowding at such densities.

Different species

The main message to remember here is that plant centres or densities do not relate directly to published plant spreads. The spread is used only as guideline information. This is particularly important when associating plants of different species, where overlaps are not only desirable but affordable.

▲ **Planting densities can vary** considerably depending on the effect you wish to achieve. Santolinas in their natural form will form a wide, rounded cushion of foliage and flower.

DIY DESIGN

Access to deep borders

- Deep or large planting areas generate maximum impact in a small garden, but they do need to be readily accessible for maintenance and upkeep.
- Stepping stones can be added strategically through the planting beds and will not impinge too much visually.
- A maintenance path at the rear of a planting bed, especially if it has a hedge as a backdrop, can provide hidden access to both the plants and the hedge.
- Access paths can be simple and low-cost, such as those made from timber-edged gravel. Tall planting towards the rear of the planting bed should hide the path altogether in most or all seasons of the year.

▲ **Seedheads of ornamental onions** remain decorative as they dry over the early summer and can be retained as a decorative feature.

1. *Allium hollandicum* 'Purple Sensation' is a favourite late spring bulb with tall, purple, spherical flowerheads that emerge through perennials and grasses.

2. The decorative thistle flowers of sea holly (*Eryngium*), such as *E. planum* 'Blaukappe', work well interplanted with finer grasses such as *Stipa tenuissima*.

3. Another interplanting favourite is towering, transparent *Verbena bonariensis*. Plant this among taller grasses such as purple moor grass (*Molinia caerulea*) or reed grass (*Calamagrostis*).

4. Ornamental onions (*Allium*) have been used here en masse among ferns as an underplanting to a spectacular, contrasting floral display by laburnum and wisteria.

Interplanting

Plant spacing can also be adjusted when interplanting, that is using plants as transitory accent ones or fillers, which require space for growth for a relatively short time during their life cycles.

Bulbs for example take up very little space, because their stems rise through other surrounding plants. Ornamental onions (*Allium*), quamash (*Camassia*) and tulips would fall into this category, because they die back as the growing season progresses. Foxgloves (*Digitalis*), *Verbena bonariensis*, foxtail lily (*Eremurus*) and some sea hollies (*Eryngium*) also work

well as fillers. The growth cycles and flowering times of species used for interplanting need to be considered before planting combinations are compiled.

Block planting

If you are wanting to have larger areas of the same species, then it is easier to dispense with individual circles once you have determined the necessary plant spacings or density. Measure out your overall border size on graph paper and then indicate plant spacings at grid intersections, so that you can assess how many plants you need for a given area.

Planting profiles

Before opening any reference books or nursery catalogues it is a good idea to work through a planting profile exercise for your garden. This allows you to produce a planting specification, so you will know what planting type, seasonal interest, height or flower colour you will be searching for in the reference sources.

This plant profile information then needs to be combined with more practical research on your soil type and its pH; the orientation of your garden and how sun and shade affect it; exposure to wind (especially important in coastal or elevated gardens); rainfall; the microclimate in your garden; and the impact of any existing vegetation in shading or drying out the soil.

To create a planting profile ask yourself the following questions.

What do you want your planting to do?

This is an important first consideration. If your answer is to screen views or give privacy to the garden, then you may be looking for plants of a certain height, foliage density or evergreen nature. Other functions include ground coverage, food production, perfume, wildlife interest or shade provision.

What planting types do you wish to include?

Which of trees, shrubs, climbers, hedges, perennials and annuals are most suitable for your requirements both functionally and decoratively? Or would just one or two of these planting types be more appropriate?

What style of planting is best for your needs?

Select from the planting styles described on pp174–185 and look at how each combines different plant material and types.

What is the concept or 'big idea' for your garden as a whole or for the planting in particular?

This question relates to the character, coloration and transparency of the plants you might select and to the way in which light and shade might influence the planting at different times of the day.

What is the main season of interest?

There is a temptation to try to include many different plants in order to achieve some interest all year round. This is a mistake, especially in a small garden, where space is at a premium.

It is better to choose individual plants that possess different characteristics across several seasons or to select a main season of interest, perhaps when you will use the garden most frequently. This is known as climax planting, because it has the most dramatic impact and uses the space most effectively.

Other design questions

You may want to add other items to your profile such as specifics on colour themes and combinations or textural foliage contrasts. The density or transparency of plants could also be considered, as could plant form.

Table-pruned *Morus alba* 'Platanifolia' creates vertical and textural interest as it towers above the low lines of herbs and other edible plants, mulched with moisture-retentive gravel.

PUTTING THEORY INTO PRACTICE

This exercise aims to reduce reliance on impulse plant selection and purchases. By identifying the practical and design requirements for your plot, the search for appropriate plants becomes much easier, and the concept-driven plant associations become much more coherent.

What to do

For this exercise, various criteria have been identified, including the overall concept ('let's party'), for a long, narrow border. Initially you need to pinpoint a rationale for the planting by compiling a plant profile (see p192). Based on the information in the plant profile you can then start to draw up a list of possible plants for the border.

Planting suggestions

Star or key plants: *Calamagrostis* x *acutiflora* 'Karl Foerster' – repeated, *Macleaya cordata*

Neutral or supporting flower/colour plants: *Achillea millefolium* 'Lilac Beauty', *Eryngium planum* 'Blaukappe', *Kniphofia* 'Tawny King', *Perovskia* 'Blue Spire', *Salvia nemorosa* 'Caradonna', *Sisyrinchium striatum*

Neutral or supporting foliage plants: *Panicum virgatum* 'Heavy Metal', *Stipa tenuissima*

Fillers: *Allium hollandicum* 'Purple Sensation', *Digitalis ferruginea*, *Eremurus* x *isabellinus* 'Cleopatra'

The border is to be dominated by the tall, erect reed grass (*Calamagrostis*), suggesting an informal grouping around which the party sparkles with colour and movement. Macleaya has been selected for its height and drama as well as for its flickering leaves, white-felted on the undersides. Its tall, buff-pink flowerheads will eventually echo those of the reed grass.

Background: Walls surround and protect the garden to a height of 1.8m (6ft). The border to be designed is 6m (20ft) long and 2m (6½ft) deep. A large, paved terrace runs alongside the border.

Overall concept: 'Let's party'
Maximum plant height: 3m (10ft)
Minimum plant height: 20cm (8in)
Planting types: Shrubs, perennials, grasses, bulbs
Season of interest: Late spring through to late summer
Flower colour: Blue, purple with hint of orange
Foliage colour: Green/grey-green
Texture: Mixture of bold and fine
Soil: Neutral – slightly alkaline
Orientation: South-facing

Neutral plants

The lower planting level includes the flowering perennials chosen around the colour theme of richer blues and purples: sage (*Salvia*), perovskia and yarrow (*Achillea*) spiked with sea hollies (*Eryngium*), red hot pokers (*Kniphofia*) and sisyrinchium. Crab grass (*Panicum*) and feather grass (*Stipa*) provide lively movement and finer textures. Ornamental onions (*Allium*), foxgloves (*Digitalis*) and foxtail lily (*Eremurus*) are interplanted to emerge through the lower layers for short-term impact.

Apart from the star or key plants, which are positioned first, the other plants should be grouped so as to maximize the impact of their colour and texture. The fillers can be informally sited as interesting accents.

1. *Digitalis ferruginea* produces tall, rusty apricot towers of flowers, and it is useful as a starring or neutral plant.

2. *Stipa tenuissima* captures light and air movement, and sparkles between more colourful perennials.

3. *Achillea millefolium* 'Lilac Beauty' brings delicate colour to a planting scheme. Its flat heads or plates of flowers form a good contrast against vertical stems.

4. *Eryngium planum* 'Blaukappe' combines rich blue coloration with sparkling and explosive flowerheads.

5. *Salvia nemorosa* 'Caradonna' delivers prolific and intense colour to the border, lasting throughout summer and into autumn.

6. *Kniphofia* 'Tawny King', with its vertical accents of orange and lemon, is an eye-catching, lively plant.

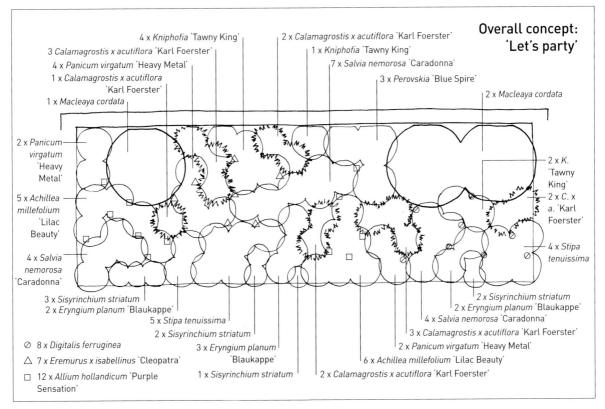

4 x *Kniphofia* 'Tawny King'
3 *Calamagrostis x acutiflora* 'Karl Foerster'
4 x *Panicum virgatum* 'Heavy Metal'
1 x *Calamagrostis x acutiflora* 'Karl Foerster'
1 x *Macleaya cordata*

2 x *Calamagrostis x acutiflora* 'Karl Foerster'
1 x *Kniphofia* 'Tawny King'
7 x *Salvia nemorosa* 'Caradonna'
3 x *Perovskia* 'Blue Spire'
2 x *Macleaya cordata*

**Overall concept:
'Let's party'**

2 x *Panicum virgatum* 'Heavy Metal'

5 x *Achillea millefolium* 'Lilac Beauty'

4 x *Salvia nemorosa* 'Caradonna'

2 x *K.* 'Tawny King'
2 x *C. x a.* 'Karl Foerster'
4 x *Stipa tenuissima*

3 x *Sisyrinchium striatum*
2 x *Eryngium planum* 'Blaukappe'
5 x *Stipa tenuissima*
2 x *Sisyrinchium striatum*
3 x *Eryngium planum* 'Blaukappe'
1 x *Sisyrinchium striatum*

2 x *Sisyrinchium striatum*
2 x *Eryngium planum* 'Blaukappe'
4 x *Salvia nemorosa* 'Caradonna'
3 x *Calamagrostis x acutiflora* 'Karl Foerster'
2 x *Panicum virgatum* 'Heavy Metal'
6 x *Achillea millefolium* 'Lilac Beauty'
2 x *Calamagrostis x acutiflora* 'Karl Foerster'

⊘ 8 x *Digitalis ferruginea*
△ 7 x *Eremurus x isabellinus* 'Cleopatra'
□ 12 x *Allium hollandicum* 'Purple Sensation'

GARDEN STARS OR GARDEN NEUTRALS?

The stars possess special attributes such as spectacular flowers, decorative bark or a specific architectural form. The neutral plants provide mainly foliage and can be used as a contrast to the more extrovert stars.

TREES

Stars: *Magnolia* x *soulangeana* [1], *Betula nigra* [2]

Neutrals: *Ilex aquifolium*, *Ligustrum lucidum*

PERENNIALS

Stars: *Phlomis russeliana* [3], *Eryngium agavifolium*, *Macleaya cordata*.

Neutrals: *Hemerocallis* [4], *Persicaria amplexicaulis* 'Alba'

GRASSES

Stars: *Pennisetum alopecuroides* 'Hameln', *Calamagrostis* x *acutiflora* 'Karl Foerster' [5], *Miscanthus sinensis* 'Malepartus'

Neutrals: *Deschampsia cespitosa* 'Goldtau', *Hakonechloa macra* [6]

WETLAND

Stars: *Rodgersia aesculifolia* [7], *Osmunda regalis*, *Zantedeschia aethiopica*

Neutrals: *Sagittaria sagittifolia* [8], *Blechnum spicant*

SHRUBS

Stars: *Hydrangea quercifolia* Snow Queen, Philadelphus 'Belle Etoile' [9], *Callicarpa bodinieri* var. *giraldii* 'Profusion'

Neutrals: *Buxus sempervirens* [10], *Pittosporum tenuifolium*

Making design statements

Plants can be loosely grouped by their relative charisma. As not all of them can be stars within the garden, some (often termed general or neutral) plants are used to give depth and background to the more exciting ones. Examples of neutral plants are hedges such as box (*Buxus*) or yew (*Taxus baccata*), which provide a backdrop to colourful plants or bold foliage. Small-leaved plants such as laurustinus (*Viburnum tinus*), hebe, Mexican orange blossom (*Choisya*) or grasses such as *Stipa tenuissima* also fall into this category. Without them the livelier stars would create a cacophony, grabbing attention at every turn and overwhelming the mind visually.

Starring plants

Any such design statements need to be made with care, so the stars are positioned appropriately to reflect their best characteristics. These plants often grow to an impressive height and stature, their form is architectural or unusual, their foliage bold and particularly decorative, and their flowers especially colourful or unusual. In addition branches or stems might display particular colorations or textures.

Several options

Position star plants singly so they give punctuation to the planting scheme, or else plant them in structured groups within your plant associations. They can also be used at key points within the garden – perhaps as the focus of the main view from the house or at the junction of paths to emphasize a particular change of direction.

Star plants are invaluable when set alongside a seat, too, or related to a piece of sculpture, to give focus.

Planting for reduced maintenance

Throughout the design and selection process for your garden, it is essential that realistic goals are set for the maintenance and long-term active gardening of your plot. Even in small gardens, the complexity and quantity of planting can be difficult to manage.

If you work full time or have a young family, for example, time for gardening will be limited. You therefore need to be aware of how much gardening time is possible within your schedule and then attempt to match plant selection and design combinations to suit that time frame. Such an approach should lead to a more successful end result. If in doubt start with simple and easy plant choices. You can always increase the complexity at a later stage.

Trees

Trees are relatively easy to care for unless poor plant selection means that they grow out of hand or are already overmature. Trees such as gum trees (*Eucalyptus*) are extremely fast growers and can develop into a full-sized tree in less than 10 years. Robinias have light, transparent foliage, which is ideal for a small space, but its brittle branches can be a disadvantage.

All trees – whether evergreen or deciduous – are constantly losing foliage, flower petals, seeds or berries and even fine branches across the year, so need some basic upkeep. However deciduous trees lose all their leaves in one season, and it takes time to remove all the leaf litter off the ground. The leaves can also block drains and gutters and will need space set aside if you wish to let the foliage rot down into leaf mulch.

Shrubs

Although some shrubs are evergreen and some deciduous, their leaf drop will be less significant than larger-

▲ **Plant with sufficient density** to cover the soil. This will reduce or eliminate competition from weeds and enhance the visual impact from massed texture and colour.

canopied trees. Other than that, shrubs are relatively low-maintenance plants until they start to fill out or grow too large. To some extent this can be anticipated in your initial shortlist of plants, but many shrubs still need pruning at least once a year to keep them healthy and in good shape or to optimize flowering for the following year. Certain forms of roses require additional pruning too. As with many plants it is the timing of the cutting back that is important.

▲ **Paved surfaces** and dense but simple planting can significantly reduce regular maintenance tasks, allowing you more time to sit and enjoy the garden.

 A combination of geotextile and gravel mulching will minimize weed infestation. Planting densities can then be reduced to reveal the form of each plant or association.

Hedges

These are often dismissed as high-maintenance features within a garden, yet they require very little attention. Trimming for most species should be done only once or twice a year, but this needs to be at regular intervals. Some hedges such as x *Cuprocyparis leylandii* grow out of hand quickly, and maintenance is then more problematic (see p121).

Hedges planted along boundaries need careful thought, because access will be needed on the neighbour's side to keep all parts of the hedge balanced. Higher barriers such as pleached hedges (see p126) will also need ladder access for trimming.

Perennials

Perennials are varied in their maintenance requirements. In cool-temperate areas, stems do not often become woody and self-supporting, unlike in warmer regions, so some taller species may need staking as the growing season progresses.

Some perennials will benefit from an early summer 'haircut' back to near ground level. This encourages plants to flower for a second time in that growing season. Others should be divided every 2–3 years to maintain their vigour.

Note those perennials that self-seed easily, because they may grow to dominate the garden. The easiest way to reduce maintenance is to choose species that remain in well-behaved clumps and to avoid vigorous growers and self-seeders. The most vigorous and invasive species will require regular attention to prevent them taking over and outcompeting neighbouring plants.

It is accepted practice now to leave the majority of perennials standing through the winter months. This provides a food source for birds. In late winter they can be cut back to just above ground level, allowing the whole growth cycle to start afresh. In a small garden it may be difficult to dispose of the resulting vegetation if your compost bin is already overfull (see p216). However your local authority may have a green waste collection.

Grasses

Some grasses also self-seed and need careful selection in the same way as perennials. Their maintenance needs are also similar.

◄ **Container-grown plants** and lawns often require the most maintenance. Consider carefully whether they realistically meet your criteria for available time for gardening.

Annuals

Once growth is underway, annuals require little attention until they die back at the end of the growing season. It may be necessary at this stage to replace them with a winter bedding crop or just keep the ground clear ready for resowing next spring. The maintenance of the bare soil in a weed-free condition is essential for the success of each year's display.

As a general rule, bare soil is the garden owner's enemy, because this represents an open invitation for weed invasion. Weed seed can be present in the existing soil and burst into life once light, heat and moisture are available. Weed seeds can also be introduced through manures and compost, especially if homemade.

Instead of using seeds, annuals can be purchased as plug plants early in the season. They are then grown on, but this entails quite a bit of work too.

Importance of mulches

Gravel is a useful mulch for beds and borders as well as a covering for paths and other surfaces, because on the whole it reduces maintenance and helps with moisture retention. When gravel is laid over a geotextile layer, weed growth can be suppressed, but all weeds need to be removed before such a surface is constructed. Wind-blown seed will still invade the gravel and needs to be regularly removed.

Other mulches such as spent mushroom compost and bark mulch can also help in the same way.

Density of planting

Increasing the density of planting is another way to reduce weed growth, because there will be less bare soil and more competition from other plants. Soil preparation and clean, weed-free conditions before planting are key to reducing persistent weeds.

The more complex the planting palette you select, however, the more challenging its maintenance will be. In this respect, cottage gardens (see p175) or English flower gardens (see p178) equate to a higher-maintenance requirement than a Minimalist (see p184) or sustainable planting (see p185). One way to mimimize this effect is to select plants that require the same or similar conditions.

Lawns

Although lawns are versatile and flexible in their shape and uses, such planted surfaces are not always suitable for small gardens, especially those in dense urban centres. Many small spaces are shaded, and even though there are lawn species mixes that are designed for shade the sward will inevitably be weak and often patchy in quality because of the lack of sun.

Of more concern is the amount of use the lawn is likely to receive, because heavy wear kills off lawn grass and compacts the ground, making re-establishment difficult.

Small lawns can potentially consume more gardening time than most other planting types. Another drawback is that scarce storage space is required for the lawnmower. Paved surfaces, which offer flexible usage, counterbalanced by rich and dynamic planting provide a much more effective combination in a small garden.

If you still want to include a lawn, position a paved mowing edge or trim around the lawn, just slightly lower than the lawn surface. The mower can then trim the lawn edges, thus saving time and equipment for this task.

Productive gardens

The productive garden is for the serious gardener in terms of maintenance requirements, especially if your entire garden is devoted to edible crops (see pp212–215).

Herbs are probably the easiest productive plants to grow because many thrive in hot, dry conditions. However if you intend to grow several crops, then watering, feeding, composting, pest control, supports, weeding, pruning and harvesting will all demand your energies.

The likely predominance of shade in a small garden and its limited size can also make it difficult to grow crops successfully. The rental of an allotment might provide a more effective, sun-filled space in which to grow a wider range of fruit, vegetables and herbs.

Vegetable gardens can be decorative and colourful as well as productive. Organize the crops to maximize textural contrast, and interplant or associate productive plants with more decorative species.

PLANTING FOR PRIVACY

In this long, narrow garden the opportunity has been taken to establish a series of separate spaces. Planting has been used to define and structure the various rooms, with paving or lawn providing surface treatments.

Height and increased scale are provided by bold specimen plants such as Montezuma pine. Its draped and transparent needles cast little shade, while the veiling character of the tree is beguiling and fascinating.

Elsewhere the bold character in the planting is continued with the hot flower colours and veined leaves of cannas or with the glossy richness of bananas (*Musa*) and tetrapanax. Other smaller, decorative plants fill the spaces in-between, with visual and horticultural richness. Containers have been used to add eye-catching highlights to the area.

Boundaries

Boundary planting is dense and succeeds in disguising the exact size and extent of the garden. The overall composition succeeds by a visual link to the mature planting in neighbouring gardens and seems to expand the available space.

Individual areas

Blocks of planting have been introduced in order to break up the garden into a series of smaller spaces. Planting is dense and often tall and bold in character, with colourful exotics included for summer interest. The overall effect is magical and enticing.

▶ **Clever use has been made** of a tree canopy from a neighbouring garden to expand the space and height visually, thereby disguising the true size of the plot.

Design ideas to take home

- Planting has been used confidently to create structure and atmosphere.
- The Montezuma pine provides a structural focal point in the centre of the garden.
- Planting works effectively to disguise boundaries and offer privacy and shelter.
- Bold, textural plants including cannas and bananas are supplemented by smaller, colourful additions.
- Use of borrowed planting and scenery from neighbours, as well as diffusion of the actual boundaries by plants, make the garden appear larger.

... a backdrop of voluptuous textures conjures an outdoor dining oasis...

SECLUDED STYLE

The spidery branches of the elegant Montezuma pine (*Pinus montezumae*) (1) dominate this secluded terrace in a small suburban garden.

The main structural planting is augmented by seasonal colour from the cannas (2), geraniums (*Pelargonium*) and palms.

Coleus 'Trusty Rusty', *Astelia chathamica* 'Silver Spear' and *Fatsia japonica* provide additional colour and foliage interest in the background (3).

The paving and furniture (4) is subdued in colour to allow the foliage composition to dominate the scene.

◀ **Repeat plantings of succulents** in a series of small, terra-cotta pots create an eye-catching focal point on this poolside shelf.

SMALL GARDEN

UPKEEP

Gardens are living ecosystems that develop and change over time. They compete for attention with many other attractions – work, family, leisure and social time – all of which must be balanced. Assess where the garden sits in your hierarchy and how much time you can give it.

The 'no-maintenance' garden does not really exist, but it is possible to balance a lower maintenance level with a busy way of life.

What is certain is that gardens and plants respond to nurture, and the process of gardening can be therapeutic, relaxing and distracting, with its seasonal cycle of growth. It offers rewards with a sense of wellbeing that few other experiences match.

15 ways to... simplify your gardening

5. Minimize weeding

Weed seeds are often blown into the garden, so clearing weeds can be a never-ending maintenance task. Raised beds and containers filled with fresh potting compost will start off being weed-free. However you still need to check such planters regularly for perennial and wind-blown weed infestation.

1. Avoid mowing

Because lawns require regular and generally more maintenance than other plants, paving is a useful, low-maintenance alternative. Grass can be particularly problematic in shaded conditions, where weaker growth means the sward is prone to moss and weed invasion.

2. Aim for a carpet of cover

Open soil can be densely planted either with low and compact ground cover or with perennials that will grow together to form a carpet of planting. Once established this reduces the ability of weeds to germinate.

3. Apply mulches

Thick mulches on the surface of planted areas retain moisture within the soil beneath while also reducing the chances of weed infestation. The soil should be moist, warm and as weed-free as possible before the mulch is applied to the surface.

4. Use geotextile fabric

Geotextiles are woven fabrics that can be used as a membrane beneath a gravel or woodchip mulch. They prevent weed growth from the soil below, although slits can be cut in them through which plants can grow. The material is permeable, so moisture can pass through.

6. Hoe lightly

'Little and often' is a useful adage for the gardener. Regular hoeing or light cultivation in planted areas will disturb or remove weeds before they start to flower and go to seed. This is a much easier way to control weed growth than leaving the garden untended for a long period.

7. Intervene early

In the quieter months of the year, from late autumn to early spring, it is useful to cultivate the soil and remove weeds when growth is slow or plants are dormant. Time invested in this period will significantly reduce your workload through the main growing season.

10. Buy long-lasting materials

Where possible select hard materials for longevity. The replacement and upkeep of low-cost materials will, over time, prove more costly than the initial outlay on higher-quality ones.

of plants. Typically prolific, self-seeding species or vigorous and overcompetitive growers will outcompete more benign species, and so require much more care to keep their growth in check.

11. Reduce complexity

Keen gardeners are frequently avid collectors of plants, seeing each new species as a fascinating horticultural challenge. By restricting yourself to a simple planting palette you can ease maintenance tasks, especially if your plants require the same or similar management techniques.

12. Plant perennials

Herbaceous perennials and most ornamental grasses have a manageable and predetermined size. Their growth pattern is predictable and much more manageable than that of shrubs and trees, which tend to grow larger within a variable size range.

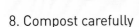

8. Compost carefully

Although the composting of plant and other organic materials is to be encouraged, ensure that you are not adding perennial weeds to your bin or heap. They will often persist in the mixture and will proliferate once you return the compost to the ground, creating even more work.

9. Opt for sustainable planting

Garden maintenance tasks can be reduced by the careful selection

13. Keep water cool

By selecting a water feature in the form of a fountain with an underground storage reservoir there is less likelihood that the water will overheat, promoting unwanted algal bloom, which can choke and stagnate the water. Also, if adding plants to a pond or pool it is advisable to choose less vigorous species to prevent mass colonization.

14. Check plant needs

Choose plant species that are suitable for the conditions that prevail in your garden rather than try to change local conditions or plant species in an alien environment. Soil pH, drainage, shade and wind turbulence should all be taken into account in plant selection.

15. Use paint-free surfaces

Brick and stone may need cleaning occasionally, but painted surfaces require much more care as well as repainting. Access could prove difficult once planting has matured. Generally natural materials need less maintenance than man-made ones.

Planning your garden's seasonal tasks

Maintenance is part of the ongoing cycle of tending and enjoying a garden. Without regular attention plants become unruly or die back, and weeds take over. Regular intervention will mean that tasks are minimized and much more controllable. They become part of a regular routine that you can more effectively build into your day-to-day living.

Regular upkeep

Generally, maintenance tasks are either carried out on a calendar basis – perhaps monthly or seasonally – or as a list of specific tasks that can focus on individual plants, plant associations or features such as ponds.

A seasonal approach will help you to understand the growth patterns and life cycle of the garden, and you can always add more specific information about special plants or tasks as you start to work in the garden.

Coming to life

It is important to note that plants tend to be dormant in temperatures lower than 6°C (42°F). These lower temperatures of late autumn through to early spring provide a chance for you to do some new planting or relocate existing plants.

As temperatures rise in late spring and remain high through summer and autumn you should restrict new planting and plant transplants, because water loss through the leaves (transpiration) will exceed the uptake of water through the roots.

Most plants are sold as pot-grown specimens. Each new plant therefore has a reservoir of moisture and protected roots, so its planting period can be extended.

Seed sowing

If you are planning to grow plants from seed then you need to plan ahead to account for the period of germination and early growth. Work backward from the time that you need the plants to perform, and ensure that you have the facilities to nurture their seeds at the required time of year. Many species like warmth and plenty of light in their early stages. Some will be frost tender and cannot be put outside until early summer. These plants should be protected in a glasshouse.

Bulb planting

Bulbs should be planted at key times. Although daffodils flower in spring their bulbs have to be planted in autumn to accommodate their growth cycle. However a few bulbs such as snowdrops often produce better

▲ The garden is constantly changing, and plants need regular attention by clearing away dead, crowded or unwanted growth.

results if planted 'in the green', in the period after flowering when the foliage is still evident.

Sources of advice

As well as referring to other books and the internet, you can seek information from gardeners, especially those in your area where conditions will be similar. You can add to this body of knowledge with your own observations, by keeping a notebook or diary to record how the garden performs from one year to the next.

Autumn jobs

Autumn is often deemed the end of the growth cycle, so it is an excellent time to begin your maintenance regime.

- Prepare the soil for new beds and borders by digging thoroughly and incorporating well-rotted manure or compost. The optimum time to dig will depend on your soil type, but soil temperatures should still be warm, and the ground softened by autumn rainfall.
- Start new planting to allow roots to take hold before the onset of colder winter temperatures.
- Lift and split for replanting any perennials that need increasing. This will reinvigorate a perennial clump with an empty centre too.
- Transplant small shrubs or trees if required. Larger specimens will need more careful lifting, because their root systems will be more expansive and easily damaged.
- Plant spring-flowering bulbs. Most other new plants can also go in at this time of year.
- Collect dead leaves regularly to make into leafmould. Chopping up the leaves can speed the process up. Remove leaf litter from the surface of a lawn, so it does not restrict grass growth.
- Continue to cut the lawn as long as temperatures remain above 6°C (42°F), although you should reduce the frequency of cutting and raise the height of the lawnmower blades.
- Tree and shrub canopies can be raised to let more light into the garden. Also trim hedges.

◀ **Many tasks such as bulb planting** need to be undertaken at specific times and should be worked into the gardening calendar.

▲ **Autumn is time for** clearance and planning. Use leaf litter to make leafmould, which makes a great soil improver.

Winter jobs

Winter is a quiet time for plant growth but is an ideal period for clearance, repair and preparation for the more intense periods of growth that follow.

- Plant bare-root plants in winter when the weather is good and the soil workable. Species such as roses establish well as bare-rooted specimens, and they are cheaper than pot-grown plants.
- Protect tender plants from frost and snow. Overwinter plants under glass or horticultural fleece. Protect plants on east-facing walls or those that catch the first rays of sunshine. Rapid freezing and thawing can cause plant damage.

▼ **Before pruning,** note how and when woody plants flower. Some do this on last year's wood; others flower on this year's stems.

- In freezing conditions check on pools and water features. Water expands as it freezes and can rupture pipes. Clear off any snow, which can cause structural damage to plants because of its weight. Vertical or 'fastigiate' specimens often suffer, because snow opens out their tight structure.
- Prune either to restrict the size of woody plants and climbers or to improve their health. Cut back winter-flowering species after flowering. Prune plants with winter stem interest such as dogwoods (*Cornus*) back to near ground level.
- Remove weed growth now to save time and effort later. Then leave the soil fallow to allow frost to break it down. This is useful with clay soils that are hard to dig.
- In late winter cut back perennials and grasses to just above ground level, once their decorative seedheads and general structure are in decline. Check on the species you have selected as they may have different cultural needs.
- Check gutters, downpipes and water butts for autumn leaves, which can block drainage systems, and for any winter damage.

Spring jobs

As spring arrives and temperatures rise, it is your last chance to introduce or move plants, because if soil is cultivated too much in spring and summer it loses moisture through evaporation when damp soil is brought to the surface.

- In early spring prune deciduous climbers and shrubs that flower on wood produced later in the season.
- As the temperatures rise and slugs and snails appear, take measures to control them so they do not completely destroy lush, new growth. Newly planted plants are especially vulnerable.
- Plant autumn-flowering bulbs.
- Sow annuals and plant new perennials for the summer garden. Keep frost-tender species under cover until there is little risk of frost.
- Start to mow the grass as soon as growth starts again, but keep the blade high for the first few cuts. Aerate the lawn, so air and moisture penetrate the roots better. Repair the lawn as temperatures increase.
- Mulch the soil once it is warm, moist and clear of weeds.
- Maintain ponds and pond plants. Thin out oxygenating plants, split and replant any overcrowded species and plant new arrivals. Check waterproof liners for any damage, especially after freezing.
- Check the entire garden for frost damage, which can lift plants and paving as the ice thaws and colder temperatures recede.
- Clean paving, which can be slippery underfoot after winter. Wash down and repair garden furniture.
- Plan the vegetable garden so you have a good harvest later in the year.

◄ **Overuse of lawns can** cause compaction. Aerate the soil in spring to alleviate this problem, and resow bare patches.

Kitchen garden soil needs help to stay healthy and productive, so try to make as much homemade compost as possible, for digging in winter.

Summer jobs

Summer should be a good time to relax in the garden and watch flowers, foliage and fruit progress through their main cycles of growth.

- If you have weeded regularly in spring, weed growth in summer should be removable by hand.
- With the exception of tender annuals, try to keep all planting to a minimum. This reduces the need for watering during these warmer, drier months.
- Generally, cut lawns closer as summer progresses, but if drier conditions prevail keep the grass longer to help preserve moisture. Lawns reliant on regular watering or irrigation will often collapse during drought, because their roots are closer to the surface.
- Deadhead regularly to encourage the production of new flowers. This applies especially to roses and many perennials. Some perennials will flower again if they are cut back after their first flowering.
- Trim hedges in early to midsummer after the early flush of growth, but before doing so check that birds are no longer nesting there. Some hedges may need only one trim each year; cut back others more often, especially if a well-clipped, formal look is to be maintained.
- Prune any climbers and shrubs that have finished flowering. Tie in and train the new growth of climbers.
- Harvest soft fruit, vegetables and herbs from the garden.
- Prune trained fruit, especially cordons or espaliered specimens, in late summer or early autumn.
- Shade and ventilate the glasshouse to prevent it overheating as light and heat levels increase.
- If you are watering the garden do this after sundown, to minimize evaporation. Use stored rainwater as much as possible to reduce reliance on the mains supply.

The productive garden

Interest in how to grow fruit and vegetables has increased dramatically over recent years. In a small garden it can be quite a challenge to fit in crops alongside ornamental colour and visual interest. Therefore you may decide it is worth devoting the entire garden to edible planting.

Basic needs

A glasshouse and cold frames are invaluable in getting the season off to a good start. Seeds can be started there and young plants grown on until the weather is suitable for them to be transplanted into the garden.

Crops in a small space

In really small areas it is good to grow herbs that can have their leaves harvested regularly over the summer months, and they will respond with new growth. They demand good light and warmth, and thrive in pots or window boxes. Species native to the Mediterranean regions are accustomed to dry conditions and do not need to be watered too regularly.

Smaller herbs such as chives and thyme work well in a pot and also thrive in a gravel garden.

Other crops to consider are rocket and cut-and-come-again salad leaves. Spinach, lettuces, pak-choi and chard respond well to frequent harvesting, and chard has decorative stems and leaves. Sow these vegetables in spring for summer eating, and again in midsummer for a late-summer or early-autumn crop.

Garlic is a good basic ingredient for most cooking. It is best planted from mid-autumn to early winter and then harvested as the leaves wither during midsummer.

Crops for larger beds

Where space permits, larger productive beds can be introduced. Soft fruits such as raspberries, which can cope with partial or light shade, and strawberries can be considered either in beds or containers.

Climbers such as runner beans, which provide height and colour as well as an edible crop, can be trained up a trellis or other support. Figs enjoy the warmth and protection of south-facing walls. Taller herbs such as fennel are also useful.

Home-grown potatoes and tomatoes are delicious, yet it may be worth considering varieties that are

---

DIY DESIGN

Watering techniques

- An automatic watering system can save water, as it delivers regular, measured irrigation. Plan its layout to reduce the impact of the pipe system within the garden. Securing a pipe in a small container can be fiddly.
- Large pots can be fitted with individual water reservoirs.
- Water well when establishing your garden, because the new plants are especially vulnerable to high temperatures and dry conditions before the root systems develop fully.
- Do not overwater, as plants will become too dependent on artificial watering, and roots will remain shallow.
- Water in the evening when temperatures are lower and evaporation will be minimal.

▲ **Regular crop patterns** are visually pleasing and functional. Ensure good access to the crops for watering, tending and harvesting.

unusual or difficult to obtain. Often the harvesting time of more common varieties coincides with their greater availability and lower price in the shops. Plant potato tubers in spring or summer for winter harvesting. Sow tomatoes in spring for summer and early-autumn harvesting.

Parsnips are slow to germinate and mature. In a small garden they can be interplanted with faster-maturing salad crops.

Crop rotation

You must rotate your crops each year in order to keep the soil healthy and reduce the threat from pests and diseases. Plan the planting positions in winter as you prepare the ground for planting. Divide your plants into four basic groups – root crops (carrots, parsnips), the brassica family (cabbages, Brussels sprouts, radishes), legumes (peas, beans) and miscellaneous vegetables (potatoes, leeks, spring onions, garlic, tomatoes, salad leaves). Plant each group in a different area in a four-year rotation.

Crops for every season

Spring – spring onions, cabbages, parsnips, radish

Summer – herbs, peas, beans, carrots, garlic, potatoes, tomatoes, salad leaves, strawberries, raspberries

Autumn – sweet peppers and chilies (under glass), apples and pears, potatoes

Winter – leeks, cabbages, Brussels sprouts, parsnips

▲ **Vegetable gardens** can also include decorative plants such as pot marigolds (*Calendula*, shown). Some vegetables have ornamental properties of their own.

Crops under glass

If you have the benefit of glass protection then more tender vegetables such as cucumbers and peppers can be attempted. Once you gain experience you can start to experiment with more unusual foods. Winter salads and herbs such as basil can also be grown in a glasshouse.

Fruit bushes and trees

Seasonal favourites such as blackberries can be wall trained to make maximum use of space in a small garden. Sunny walls can be exploited for peaches or apricots if you feel a little more ambitious.

Fruit trees are available in a wide range of sizes and forms. Dwarf ones are best in a small garden, when space is tight; they are also easy to harvest. Stepover apple trees, in which the stems are trained horizontally, low down, can be used to edge a border or path. Espalier or cordon apples and pears work well when trained against

a garden wall or trellis, and they take up little border space.

Blurring the boundary

Soft fruits such as raspberries, gooseberries and red- or blackcurrants, as well as rhubarb, tolerate some shade, and they also look good when planted within more decorative borders. It may be necessary to cover them with netting to protect the fruit from birds, but this can detract from the display. For an early crop, rhubarb can be forced by covering emerging stems with a pot.

Beetroot foliage works well in a decorative border, and runner beans will also add height and splashes of colour. Herbs can be grown in this way, too, rather than in a specific area.

Conversely, decorative planting can find its way into the vegetable garden not simply for decoration but also as a way of attracting beneficial insects. The delicate fronds of dill will enhance any border, and these plants also attract aphid-eating hoverflies. Fennel will do the same task. Use decorative, edible nasturtium flowers for a blaze of colour and to attract caterpillars away from edible crops.

Sowing

Spring is the main time to sow vegetables and plant fruit for summer and autumn harvesting. Growing plants from seed is rewarding and economical. Tender vegetables can be sown under glass or indoors, with more hardy vegetables sown directly in the ground outdoors.

Some plants need bottom heat to assist germination, and small propagators are available that can be accommodated on a sunny windowsill if you do not have a glasshouse. Transparent covers with vents allow temperature and humidity to be controlled. Herbs, such as basil, and vegetables, such as celery and peas, germinate well in propagators. You can even crop their leaves before these vegetables are fully mature, for a tasty salad dish.

Thin seedlings carefully and regularly, because they always grow clumped together. Try to retain the strongest plant in any clump and discard or eat the weaker seedlings, or replant them elsewhere to grow on.

Many annuals and vegetables are also sold as young plants or plugs. These offer the joys of home-grown

▶ **Crops such as strawberries** thrive in
containers, which restrict access for slugs.
Use them to decorate the terrace.

produce without the need for sowing
seeds or a propagator. The choice of
varieties is more limited than when
buying seed but the end result is just
as tasty. Initially you will need to grow
them on in a protected area.

Planting out

Once young plants in a protected
environment are large enough to go in
the garden, gradually harden them off.
Initially leave them outside during the
day and bring them in at night. After a
week or so, leave them out at night as
well, provided there is no risk of frost.
Then plant them in an appropriate
spot in the garden to grow on.

   Once crops have been harvested it
is time to cultivate and manure beds
as the annual cycle starts again.

DIY DESIGN

Container-grown citrus plants

- Fruit such as citrus work well in portable pots, because
  they need to be moved to a protected area for winter.
- Terra cotta is a good choice for the pot, because it
  echoes the Mediterranean character of citrus fruit.
  The tree needs to be well watered, so ensure its pot is
  as large as possible and has a reservoir. The container
  must drain well however.
- Dwarf forms of citrus crop well and are ideal for a small
  space. They are grafted, so cut off any new shoots
  produced low down from the rootstock.
- Position the plant for maximum sun and warmth.
- Apart from limes, pick fruits once no longer green.

Good housekeeping

Any garden needs a certain amount of housekeeping to ensure it always looks neat and tidy. Pests can cause havoc by nibbling leaves or destroying whole plants, so these need to be controlled too.

In a small garden, processing and getting rid of even a small amount of garden waste can pose difficulties. There may be nowhere to store it, and it may have to be transported through the house for street collection.

Compost and compost bins

The best way to deal with garden waste is to compost it, in a bin or heap, but this is sometimes not possible if space is really tight in a garden.

Homemade compost is a very useful substance, and is an invaluable way of recycling your green waste into a nutritious soil improver. When fully rotted, it can be spread across your beds and borders as a mulch or dug into the soil in generous amounts to prevent soil exhaustion.

Compost bins are available in a range of materials, sizes and styles to suit different needs. If you build your own bin, make sure the main structure is sturdy and that air can circulate through its sides, which will help with the rotting process. To assist with drainage, make sure the bin is positioned on bare soil, not on a hard surface.

If you have space, and a ready supply of fallen deciduous leaves, it is worth making your own leafmould. This is an excellent soil improver and simply involves stuffing the leaves into bin bags, poking holes into their sides for aeration, and leaving them for a season or two until the leaves have crumbled into a fine, earthy substance. If you do not have space, then you can mix deciduous leaves into a regular compost heap.

For a very small garden, you can use a wormery to make a nutrient-rich, liquid plant food from ordinary kitchen waste. Worm bins, however, are unsuitable for dealing with much in the way of garden waste.

Materials to compost

You need a balanced mixture of carbon-rich materials, such as hedge trimmings and shredded paper, and softer, nitrogen-rich waste, such as lawn clippings and dead flowerheads and foliage.

Avoid weeds and any diseased material, because they will spread

DIY DESIGN

The composting process

- Compost is a good material to add to soil, because it feeds the soil and improves its structure and texture.
- The compost bin should have a lid to help insulation and a minimum volume of 1 cu m (35 cu ft) in order to generate enough heat for rotting and decomposition.
- Whether timber or plastic, the bin should be as robust as possible, and air should be able to circulate all around the bin and compost. Turn the contents at least once a year to assist the rotting process.
- Once the material has broken down, it should be spread on beds and borders. It is simplest to do this when the garden is at its barest, that is in winter.

▶ **Refuse and compost bins** are often hidden behind simple timber trellis or plant-covered screens to reduce their visual impact within the garden.

through the compost and continue to cause problems when you add the material back to the garden soil.

Kitchen waste, such as peelings and leftover salads and tea bags, can also be added. Never compost cooked food, because it will attract vermin.

Alternatives to compost

If you are not making your own compost, a number of other soil improvers are available to home gardeners. The most common is manure, but it must be well rotted and free of weed seeds; most garden centres sell prebagged manure that is ready to use.

Another common material is soil conditioner made from garden waste collected by the council. This is done on an industrial scale, and the end result sold back to home gardeners. It tends to be of medium to low fertility, but unlike homemade compost it contains far fewer weed seeds, because they are destroyed by the higher heat levels generated in industrial-sized heaps.

Organic mulches, such as woodchips or cocoa shells, are not strictly soil improvers, but they do begin to behave as such as they gradually rot down on top of the soil.

Common pests

Pests can be a major nuisance. It is not possible to eradicate them, but they can be kept under control.

Slugs and snails
Young plants and new shoots of certain plants are particularly vulnerable.

Patrol with a torch on mild, damp evenings, when these pests are most active, to identify which plants are being attacked. Concentrate your pest-killing activities on these plants. The various control methods differ in effectiveness. Use slug pellets sparingly, and only on vulnerable plants.

Aphids
Also known as blackfly or greenfly, these sap-suckers can distort and disfigure plants. In a small garden, it is quite an easy task to wash or rub off any infestations with your fingers.

Vine weevils and caterpillars
Pot-grown plants are particularly susceptible to vine weevils, which feed on plant roots undeterred by their predators that lurk in open garden soil. Chemical and biological controls are available. Destroy the adult weevils whenever you see them.

Caterpillars feed on leaves and flower buds. Light infestations can be controlled by hand; heavier ones may result in the complete destruction of a plant if not controlled by spraying. Vulnerable plants such as cabbages can be protected with netting.

▲ **Ladybirds are beneficial garden visitors,** because they feed on sap-sucking aphids and reduce their infestations.

▲ **Slugs are destructive pests,** damaging seedlings and new shoots. Trap or bait them, or remove them by hand on a night patrol.

THE LOW-MAINTENANCE GARDEN

Gardens vary considerably in their level of upkeep, and this one has been designed so it is minimal. Therefore plants have been chosen to match the prevailing gardening conditions rather than attempt to introduce artificial environments that might suit a different range of plants.

Paul Dracott has here designed a small garden for visual interest and pleasure without a regular input of upkeep and management.

Lawns however do need constant upkeep, and their removal can significantly free up time. Paving or decking are other options, while artificial lawns are available in a wide range of textures and colours. Moisture-retentive mulches such as gravels and cobbles laid on the soil will also reduce weed colonization.

More low-maintenance tips

Plant for sculptural effect, relying on Mediterranean-type species for their drought tolerance. Use hard materials or a piece of sculpture to bring colour and vitality into the garden, or plant a small number of perennials and ornamental grasses. These need little regular maintenance, often requiring only a cutback once a year.

◀ **The use of hard materials** instead of a lawn reduces maintenance. Minimalist planting can be used to compensate for the loss of grass.

Maintenance ideas to take home

- Consider upkeep implications when designing any aspect of a garden.
- Paved surfaces should be cleaned and sometimes weeded.
- Decking, which can been allowed to silver with age, should have a weed-suppressing mat beneath it.
- Gravel can be used as a mulch on the planting beds. When laid over a geotextile mat this technique can significantly reduce weeding and also help to conserve moisture in the soil.
- Perspex or glass screens require regular cleaning for optimum light.
- Many grasses and perennials need to be cut back in late winter, to allow for new growth in spring and summer. This can significantly change the appearance of the garden.
- Shrubs need pruning for general health and vigour as well as to restrict their size and spread or reshape them.

... transparent colours enrich the textures in this easy-care garden...

A FEAST OF TEXTURES

A suspended chair (1) provides a focal point for relaxation, moving gently in any breeze.

Paving (2) in large, oblong blocks emphasizes the width of the garden, introducing a horizontal, linear pattern, while the decking (3) echoes this pattern in a softer, silvered tone.

Planting areas (4) are mulched with gravel to reduce weed growth. Grasses such as blue tussock grass (*Poa labillardierei*), feather grass (*Stipa*) and fescue (*Festuca*) are supported by lilyturf (*Liriope*) and elephant's ears (*Bergenia*), and the dramatic foliage of sun-loving agave. Silver-foliage shrubs such as sea buckthorn (*Hippophae rhamnoides*) and coyote willow (*Salix exigua*) add to the scene.

◀ **Translucent perspex screens** break up the space, reduce the impact of boundaries and increase the scale and depth of the garden.

Acknowledgements

I would firstly like to thank my wife Barbara for her patience through the writing of this book, especially when I worked late into the evenings. I'm immensely grateful to commissioning editor Helen Griffin, who has been a huge support. Her dedication to timetables, programmes and deadlines has kept me on the straight and narrow. Joanna Chisholm also deserves a big thank you for understanding my intentions as she edited the text.

A special mention goes to the following people who graciously allowed us into their gardens to snoop around and photograph their inner – or perhaps I should say – outer sanctums or the gardens they had designed: Peter and Jenny Barham, John Brookes for Ronald Ingram, Andrew Fisher Tomlin, Simon and Belinda Leathes, Andy Male, Deborah Nagan, Charlotte Noar for John Hood, Maria Örnberg for Paul Mason, Michèle Osborne, Charles Rutherfoord, Tom Stuart-Smith for Anna Marrs, Victoria Summerley, Robin Williams for Maggie Guitar; and Patrick Wilson whose garden I designed.

My thanks go finally to Stephen Wooster, who brought these gardens to life with such an eye for colour and composition. Thank you also to all the photographers whose work is listed below and which brings this book to life.

PHOTOGRAPHY AND ILLUSTRATION CREDITS
(t) top (b) bottom, (l) left, (m) middle, (r) right

Andrew Wilson 12 (illustration); 14 (illustration); 38 (t); 46 (both illustrations); 131 (t); 154; 170; 181 Chris Beardshaw at RHS Tatton Park Show; 195 (illustration); 196 (6).

GAP Photos 15; GAP Photos/Mark Winwood pg186.

Garden World Images
A. James 180; **Andrea Jones** 68 The Laurent-Perrier Garden designer Tom Stuart-Smith RHS Chelsea 2008; 80 L'Occitane Garden designer James Towillis; **C. Linnett** 174 Garden Exposures 82; **J. Lilly** 75 (b) Wollerton Old Hall garden; **L. Every** 195 (3); **M. Bolton** 190 (4) Barnsley House Gardens; **N. Appleby** 74 The Chris Beardshaw Wormcast Garden 'Growing for Life' at Boveridge House; **N. Colborn** 122 (b).

Gartenart 150.

MMGI (all RHS Chelsea 2011 except *)
Marianne Majerus 8–9 Laurie Chetwood and Patrick Collins; 17 (b) Adam Frost; 21 (r) Sarah Eberle; 22–23 Bunny Guinness; 28–29 Adam Frost; 33 (t) Sarah Eberle; 41 (t) Cleve West; 48 (t) and 179 (b) Christopher Bradley-Hole*; 49 Kate Gould; 50–51 Olivia Kirk; 52 Nigel Dunnett; 46 Nigel Dunnett; 62–63 Diarmuid Gavin; 69 (b) Laurie Chetwood and Patrick Collins; 71 Jamie Dunstan; 72 Jamie Dunstan; 73 Laurie Chetwood and Patrick Collins; 83 Nigel Dunnett; 100 Robert Myers; 105 Graham Bodle; 106–107 Bunny Guinness; 123 Kate Gould; 146–147 Adam Frost; 148 (b) Paul Hervey-Brookes; 155 (b) Luciano Giubbilei; 175 Cleve West; 176 (t) Laurie Chetwood and Patrick Collins; 177 Sarah Eberle; 185 (b) Ann-Marie Powell; 185 (t) RHS Garden, Wisley, design: James Hitchmough; 187 Adam Frost; 192–193 Laurie Chetwood and Patrick Collins; 214 Anthea Guthrie; 215 (t).
Bennet Smith 48 (t) Stephen Hall; 88–89 Robert Myers; 97 (b) Kirkside of Lochty; 110–111 Jihae Hwang; 133 Jamie Dunstan; 139 Martin Cook and Bonnie Davies; 157 Thomas Hoblyn; 164–165 Marcus Barnett; 178 Marcus Barnett; 184 Diarmuid Gavin; 204–205 Laurie Chetwood and Patrick Collins.
Simon Meaker 24–25 Marney Hall; 64–65 Gillespies; 70 Heather Appleton; 98 (t) Jihae Hwang; 128–129 Stephen Hall; 161 (b) Gillespies; 201 Anthea Guthrie.

Octopus
David Sarton 2 The Laurent-Perrier Garden by Tom Stuart-Smith, RHS Chelsea 2008; 6 The Alternative Feng Shui Garden, RHS Hampton Court 2005; 21 (t) RHS Chelsea 2005, designer Andy Sturgeon; 21 (l) RHS Hampton Court 2007 Centrepoint Garden, designer Claire Whitehouse; 40 (r) The Children's Society Garden, RHS Chelsea 2008, designer Mark Gregory; 65 (b) Fleming's & Trailfinders Australian Garden, RHS Chelsea 2008; 66–67 The Daily Telegraph Garden, RHS Chelsea 2007, designers Gabriella Pape and Isabelle Van Groeningen; 77 The Chris Beardshaw Garden, RHS Chelsea 2007, designer Chris Beardshaw; 81 (t) SPANA's Courtyard Refuge, RHS Chelsea 2008, designer Chris O'Donoghue; 81 (b) Growing Together Garden, RHS Hampton 2007, designer Fiona Stephenson; 119 The Unwind Garden, RHS Hampton Court 2007, designer Mike Harvey; 134, Gabriel Ash, RHS Chelsea 2008; 136 North East England @ Home, RHS Chelsea 2008; 198 (l) Beyond the Pale, RHS Chelsea 2005, designed by Brinsbury College; 198–199 Lust for Life, RHS Chelsea 2007, designer Angus Thompson; 200 Pushing the Edge of the Square Garden, RHS Hampton Court 2005,

design Suzan Slater. **Stephen Robson** 182 Hadspen Garden. **Torie Chugg** 15 (l, m, r); 183 (t) RHS Rosemoor Garden.

The Garden Collection
Andrew Lawson 94–95; 196 (5). **Derek St Romaine** 158 (b) Garden: Glen Chantry; 188–189 Mr & Mrs Jolley, Maycotts; 143 designer Cleve West, sculpture: Johnny Woodward. **FLPA-Gary Smith** 199 (r). **Jane Sebire** 142. **John Glover** 46 (b) Butterstream, County Meath. **Liz Eddison** 12 (b); 37 designer Louise Harrison-Holland, RHS Tatton Park 2008; 85 (b); 97 (t) Harpuk Design, RHS Chelsea 2007; 104 (b) designer Marcus Barnett, Philip Nixon, RHS Chelsea 2006; 121 designer Adam Frost, RHS Chelsea 2007; 130 (r); 132 (t); 190 (1); 196 (2) designer Patrick Garland, RHS Chelsea 2002; 10–11 designer Sue Beesley, RHS Tatton Park 2007. **Marie O'Hara** 78 (b) designer Kazuyuki Ishihara; 216. **Nicola Stocken Tomkins** 30–31; 48 (b); 51 (b); 84 (b); 114–115; 130 (l); 183 (b); 189 (b); 196 (3); 211; 213. **Torie Chugg** 33 (b).

Thinkstock
Cornstock 117 (3). **Design Pics** 196 (7). **Digital Vision** 207 (l). **Hemera** 17 (t), 18 (1); 67 (l); 79 (t); 92 (b); 93 (t); 94 (b); 96 (l); 96 (r); 102–103 (b); 115 (b); 117 (4); 138; 151; 155 (t); 190 (2); 206–207; 210 (r); 212; 217 (bl); 217 (br). **iStockphoto** 10; 12 (l); 13; 18 (2); 18 (3); 18 (4); 18 (5); 18 (6); 18 (7); 19 (1); 19 (2); 19 (3); 19(4); 19 (5); 23 (b); 44 (1); 44 (2); 44 (3); 44 (4); 44 (5); 53 (bl); 54 ; 57 (t); 58; 64 (b); 65 (t); 67 (r); 76; 78 (b); 78 (t); 90; 91 (b); 91 (t); 92 (t); 93 (b); 95 (r); 98 (bl); 99; 102–103 (t); 104 (t); 112 (b); 112 (l); 113 (r); 114 (b); 117 (1); 117 (2); 120 (b); 120 (t); 131 (b); 135; 137; 140; 148 (t); 149 (b); 149 (t); 146 (b); 158 (tll); 158 (tr); 159; 160; 161 (t); 166; 167 (b); 167 (tll); 167 (tr); 168–169 (b); 171; 172 (b); 172 (t); 173; 176 (b); 179 (t); 189 (t); 190 (3); 191; 194; 195 (2); 195 (4); 195 (5); 195 (6); 196 (1); 196 (4); 197 (8); 197 (10); 206 (l); 209 (r); 210 (l); 215 (b). **Photodisc** 116; 168–169 (t). **Photos.com** 146 (b). **Zoonar** 197 (9); 209 (b)

Steven Wooster 11; 22 (b); 26–27; 26 (b); 27 (b); 30 (b); 31 (l); 31 (r); 32 (b); 34–35; 36; 38 (b); 39; 40 (l); 41 (b); 42–43; 45; 47 (t); 47 (b); 50 (b); 53 (t); 53 (br); 55; 57 (b); 59; 60; 61 (b); 69 (t); 75 (t); 84–85; 86–87; 98 (t); 108 (b); 109; 112–113; 118; 122 (t); 124–125; 126–127; 132 (b); 141; 144–145; 152–153; 162–163; 202; 202–203; 207 (r); 208–209; 217 (t); 218–219.